Understanding Buying Behaviour of Indian Families

About the book...

How do consumers make purchase decisions is a fascinating subject to be studied. Family as a conglomerate of several individuals influences the purchase of various products. The influence of family in the purchase decision-making depends upon the cultural background. Though vast literature on the subject is available on Western society, there is a dearth of material on purchase behaviour of Indian families. This book attempts to fill this gap. It provides a comprehensive analysis of the purchase behaviour of Indian households in terms of a select category of consumer durables. It makes useful suggestions for devising appropriate marketing strategies.

About the author...

Sheetal Kapoor did her B. Com. (Hons.) from the prestigious Hindu College, University of Delhi. Thereafter, she obtained her M. Com., M. Phil. and Ph. D. degrees from the University of Delhi. Dr. Kapoor has 8 years of teaching and research experience to her credit. Specialising in marketing strategies, she has published a number of articles in reputed professional journals on the subject. Presently, she is a lecturer in the Department of Commerce, Kamla Nehru College, University of Delhi.

Understanding Buying Behaviour of Indian Families

Sheetal Kapoor
Lecturer in Commerce
Kamala Nehru College
University of Delhi
New Delhi

NEW
NC
CENTURY

NEW CENTURY PUBLICATIONS
DELHI INDIA

NEW CENTURY PUBLICATIONS
34, Gujranwala Town, Part-2,
Delhi - 110 033 INDIA
Tel.: 7247805, 7138192
Fax: +91-11-7464774
E-mail: indiatax@del2.vsnl.net.in

First Published 2002

ISBN: 81-7708-027-x

Published by New Century Publications and printed at Print Line, New Delhi -110 002

PRINTED IN INDIA

Preface

An important task of any marketer is to identify and understand his customers. Knowledge about buyer's behaviour is necessary for devising an effective marketing strategy. It is an acknowledged fact that members in a family influence the decision-making process in the purchase of different products. This is particularly true for high-value items, such as consumer durable products that are used by several members in the family. Therefore, for certain product categories, the real target for the marketer is not any individual member but the family as a whole.

While developing the marketing plan, it is the family which should be considered as a unit of consumption rather than an individual. Analysis of family buying behaviour helps the marketing manager in product planning, product promotion and product pricing.

No specific study has been conducted on Indian families to examine different aspects of buying roles and how they shift for different product categories in the context of major demographic variables. The present book is an attempt to fill this vacuum. It is designed to provide a basic framework on how members in a family influence the decision-making process in the purchase of different products.

This book is based on the findings of a survey of 313 families, spread all over the metropolitan city of Delhi, who had recently purchased any of the six durable products, namely audio system, car, personal computer, refrigerator, television and washing machine.

The book is organised in 9 chapters.

Chapter 1 provides the theoretical backdrop on the family decision-making. Chapter 2 discusses the concepts as used in the literature on marketing in India and abroad. Chapter 3 introduces the research design and methodology used for the study. Chapters 4 to 8 are devoted to each of the buying roles played by family members in relation to different durable products. Thus, Chapter 4 examines the first buying role of the *initiator*. Chapter 5 analyses the role of the *influencer*. Chapter 6 studies the role of the *decider* and the extent of consultations done with other family members. Chapter 7 deals with the role of the *buyer*. Chapter 8 examines the post-purchase behaviour of the *user* members. Implications of the study for marketing strategies are discussed in Chapter 9.

I record my deep sense of gratitude to Prof. D. P. S. Verma, Department of Commerce, Delhi School of Economics, University of Delhi for generating and sustaining my interest in the field of marketing and also helping me at various stages of the writing of this book. I must express my gratitude to Prof. Y. P. Singh, Head, Department of Commerce, Delhi School of Economics, University of Delhi, for his encouragement and support. I am no less indebted to Dr. B. S. Nagi, former Director of Research, Council for Social Development, New Delhi, for his valuable guidance.

Thanks are due to Dr. Surinder J. Sharma, Principal, Kamala Nehru College, University of Delhi, for providing necessary leave from duty to complete this work.

My parents have been a constant source of inspiration and support and I take this opportunity to express my indebtedness to them. I owe a special word of appreciation for my husband, Mr. Jayant Kapoor, for his moral support and understanding during the course of this work. Lastly, a word of affection for my daughter Sukriti who provided lighter moments during long hours of work.

Delhi
June 26, 2002

Sheetal Kapoor

Contents

Preface v

List of Tables xi

1. Introduction 1-34
The Concept of Family
Functions of the Family
How Families Make Purchase Decisions
Family Decision-making
Family Life Cycle
Profile of the Selected Durable Products
Audio System Market
Car Market
The Personal Computer Market
Refrigerator Market
Colour Television Market
Washing Machine Market
Summary

2. Studies on Family Purchases: Global and the Indian Experience 35-97
Studies on Exploration of Product Categories and Family Decision-making
Studies on Investigation of Determinants of Joint Decision-making under Conflicting Goals
Studies on Changing Roles of the Wife and Children
Studies on Family Decision-making in India
Summary

3. Family Decision-making Process: An Overview **98-109**

Significance of Understanding the Family Decision-Making Process

Changing Characteristics of Indian Families

Relevance to the Marketer

Product Selection

Summary

4. Buying Roles: The Initiator **110-135**

Characteristics of the Initiator

Member-wise Status of Initiators

Initiator Member vis-à-vis the Product Purchased

Mentioning the Product's Need to a Particular Family Member

Time Taken in Actual Purchase of the Product

Reasons for the Purchase of Product

Mentioning Purchased Product's Need in the Past

Reasons for Postponing the Purchase of Product

Extent of Satisfaction from the Purchased Product

Conclusion

5. Buying Roles: The Influencer **136-187**

Characteristics of the Influencer

Member-wise Status of Influencers

Influencer Member vis-à-vis the Product Purchased

Suggestions for Technical Aspects of the Product

Technical Factors Considered by the Influencers

Extent of Consideration of Influencers' Suggestions

Brand Preference of the Influencers

Reasons for Preferring a Particular Brand

Consideration of Influecers' Brand Preference

Sources of Information

Suggestions for the Place of Purchase
Nature of Contribution of Influencers' Views:
Solicited or Voluntary
Family Members Soliciting Influencers' Views
Conclusion

6. Buying Roles: The Decider **188-211**
Characteristics of the Decider
Member-wise Status of Deciders
Decider Member vis-à-vis Product Purchased
Factors Considered While Purchasing the Product
Trade-off Among Alternative Products
Members Whose Views Were Considered by the Decider
Extent of Consultation for the Product Purchased
Financial Contribution for the Purchase of Product
Conclusion

7. Buying Roles: The Actual Buyer **212-224**
Characteristics of the Buyer
Member-wise Status of Buyers
Buyer Member vis-à-vis the Product Purchased
Buyer's Product-Rating
Family Members Accompanying the Buyer
Dealer's Opinion at the Time of Purchase
Effect of the Discussion with the Dealer
Conclusion

8. Buying Roles: The Product User **225-233**
Characteristics of the User
Member-wise Status of Users
User Member vis-à-vis the Product Purchased
Users' Satisfaction on Product Aspects

Users' Post-Purchase Satisfaction
Recommendation for the Product to Others
Conclusion

9. Implications for Marketing Strategies **234-248**
Summary of Buying Roles
Initiator
Influencer
Decider
Buyer
User
Various Implications for the Marketer
Product-Member Relationships
Intra-Family Dynamics in the Purchase of a Consumer Durable Product
Impact of Demographic Variables
Motives for the Purchase of a Product
Role of the Dealer
Post-Purchase Satisfaction

Bibliography **249-266**

Index **267-270**

List of Tables

Table 1.1: Common Terms Used in Family Research
Table 3.1: Profile of Respondents
Table 3.2: Distribution of Respondents by Family Size
Table 3.3: Distribution of Respondents by Monthly Household Income
Table 4.1: Characteristics of Initiators (Respondents)
Table 4.2: Member-wise Status of Initiators
Table 4.3: Initiator Member vis-à-vis Product Purchased
Table 4.4: Mentioning the Product's Need to a Particular Family Member
Table 4.5: Time Taken in Actual Purchase of Product
Table 4.6: Time Taken in Purchase Decision vis-à-vis Income
Table 4.7: Time Taken in Purchase Decision vis-à-vis Age of Initiators
Table 4.8: Time Taken vis-à-vis Education of Initiators
Table 4.9: Time Taken vis-à-vis Sex of Initiators
Table 4.10: Time Taken in Purchase Decision vis-à-vis Occupation
Table 4.11: Time Taken vis-à-vis Family Size
Table 4.12: Time Taken in Purchase Decision vis-à-vis Product
Table 4.13: Reasons for the Purchase of Product
Table 4.14: Mentioning Purchased Product's Need in the Past
Table 4.15: Reasons for Postponing the Purchase of Product
Table 4.16: Need specified for the Purchase of Product in Terms of Type, Features and Functions
Table 4.17: Extent of Satisfaction from the Purchased Product
Table 4.18: Time Taken in Purchase Decision vis-à-vis

Level of Needs Met
Table 5.1: Characteristics of the Influencer (Respondents)
Table 5.2: Member-wise Status of Influencers
Table 5.3: Influencer Member vis-à-vis Product Purchased
Table 5.4: Suggestions for Technical Aspects of the Product
Table 5.5: Income and the Suggestions for Technical Aspects
Table 5.6: Age and the Suggestions for Technical Aspects
Table 5.7: Education and the Suggestions for Technical Aspects
Table 5.8: Sex and the Suggestions for Technical Aspects
Table 5.9: Occupation and Suggestions for Technical Aspects
Table 5.10: Family Size and Suggestions for Technical Aspects
Table 5.11: Product and Suggestions for Technical Aspects
Table 5.12: Technical Aspects Considered
Table 5.13: Extent of Consideration of Influencers' Suggestions
Table 5.14: Income and the Extent of Consideration of Influencers' Suggestions
Table 5.15: Age and the Extent of Consideration of Influencers' Suggestions
Table 5.16: Education and the Extent of Consideration of Influencers' Suggestions
Table 5.17: Sex and the Extent of Consideration of Influencers' Suggestions
Table 5.18: Occupation and the Extent of Consideration of Influencers' Suggestions
Table 5.19: Family Size and the Extent of Consideration of Influencers' Suggestions
Table 5.20: Product and the Extent of Consideration of Influencers' Suggestions

Table 5.21: Brand Preference of the Influencers
Table 5.22: Income and the Suggestions for Brands
Table 5.23: Age and the Suggestions for Brands
Table 5.24: Education and the Suggestions for Brands
Table 5.25: Sex and the Suggestions for Brands
Table 5.26: Occupation and the Suggestions For Brands
Table 5.27: Family Size and the Suggestions for Brands
Table 5.28: Product and the Suggestions for Brands
Table 5.29: Reasons for Preferring a Particular Brand
Table 5.30: Extent to Which Preference for any Brand was Considered
Table 5.31: Income and the Extent to which Suggestions for any Brand were Considered
Table 5.32: Age and the Extent to which Suggestions for any Brand were Considered
Table 5.33: Education and the Extent to which Suggestions for any Brand were Considered
Table 5.34: Sex and the Extent to which Suggestions for any Brand were Considered
Table 5.35: Occupation and the Extent to which Suggestions for any Brand were Considered
Table 5.36: Family Size and the Extent to which Suggestions for any Brand were Considered
Table 5.37: Product and the Extent to which Suggestions for any Brand were Considered
Table 5.38: Sources of Information
Table 5.39: Suggestions for the Place of Purchase
Table 5.40: Nature of Contribution of Influencers' Views
Table 5.41: Income and Nature of Contribution of Influencers' Views
Table 5.42: Age and Nature of Contribution of Influencers' Views
Table 5.43: Education and Nature of Contribution of

Influencers' Views
Table 5.44: Sex and Nature of Contribution of Influencers' Views
Table 5.45: Occupation and Nature of Contribution of Influencers' Views
Table 5.46: Family Size and Nature of Contribution of Influencers' Views
Table 5.47: Product and Nature of Contribution of Influencers' Views
Table 5.48: Family Members Soliciting Influencers' View
Table 6.1: Characteristics of Deciders (Respondents)
Table 6.2: Member-wise Status of Deciders
Table 6.3: Decider Member vis-à-vis Product Purchased
Table 6.4: Factors Considered while Purchasing the Product
Table 6.5: trade-off among Alternative Products
Table 6.6: Views of which Family Members Considered
Table 6.7: Extent of Consultation for the Product Purchased
Table 6.8: Deciders' Degree of Consultation vis-à-vis Income
Table 6.9: Degree of Consultation vis-à-vis Age
Table 6.10: Degree of consultation vis-à-vis Education
Table 6.11: Degree of consultation vis-à-vis Sex
Table 6.12: Degree of consultation vis-à-vis Occupation
Table 6.13: Degree of Consultation vis-à-vis Family Size
Table 6.14: Determinants of Consultation with other Family Members for the Purchase of Durable Products
Table 6.15: Extent of consultation vis-à-vis Product Categories
Table 6.16: Financial Contribution for the Purchase
Table 6.17: Combinations of the Family Members who Contributed Financially
Table 7.1: Characteristics of Buyers (Respondents)
Table 7.2: Member-wise Status of Buyers

Table 7.3: Buyer Member vis-à-vis Product Purchased
Table 7.4: Buyer's Product-Rating
Table 7.5: Member Groups who went for the Purchase
Table 7.6: Dealer's Opinion at the Time of Purchase
Table 7.7: Discussion with the Dealer
Table 8.1: Characteristics of Users (Respondents)
Table 8.2: Member-wise Status of Users
Table 8.3: User Member vis-à-vis the Durable Product
Table 8.4: Users' Satisfaction on Product Aspects
Table 8.5: Users' Post-Purchase Satisfaction
Table 8.6: Recommendation for the Product to Others

1

Introduction

Despite cultural diversity, there is considerable uniformity in the structure of families in India. Cultural values inculcated during the upbringing make the Indian families different from those in the West in many ways.

Since the family plays an important part in the purchase decision-making, the real target for the marketer is not the individual but the family as a whole. In India, where joint and nuclear families co-exist, the marketer needs to focus attention not just on the individual but people defined by their positions, relationships and roles in the context of their families.

In the wake of liberalisation, media explosion and certain societal changes in India, roles of different members in a family are shifting. Thus, a substantial number of married women are working outside the house. The role of the women in this segment is undergoing a tremendous change because of the emergence of nuclear family. The voice of the woman has become stronger in the affairs of the family and there is a strong urge to relieve the housewife from the drudgery of the kitchen to perform her social, economic and family roles more effectively. The idea of the educated woman working in clerical, administrative and professional positions is no longer repugnant. In fact, there is a growing demand for educated housewives in this segment who would have some earning potential. Presently, Indian women are actively participating in the family purchase decisions with regard to all high-value items.

Kinship considerations and primary group factors continue to have a stronghold over the family and vital family purchase decisions are taken after due consideration from these groups.

With children getting more attention in a small family, there is a general willingness to meet their reasonable needs and desires to facilitate their success in life even at the cost of present hardships. Concern for the future of the next generation appears uppermost in the minds of the parents.

This chapter presents a conceptual framework essential for understanding the concept of family. The necessary theoretical backdrop is provided by a brief description of the terms used in family research, namely, family, functions of the family, and family decision-making. A profile of the six durable products selected for the study is also given.

The Concept of Family

Although 'family' seems to be an intuitive term, it is difficult to define because family composition and structure, as well as the roles played by family members are almost always in transition [1].

A family is defined by the Bureau of the Census of the U. S. as "two or more persons related by blood, marriage or adoption and living together" [2]. The area of family research considers the family as a unit of analysis. Family research attempts to describe and understand how family members interact and influence one another in terms of individual, family or household purchases [3]. Kotler asserts that there are two families in the buyer's life- the family of orientation and the family of procreation. The family of orientation consists of one's parents and siblings from where a person acquires an orientation towards religion, politics and economics, and a sense of personal ambition, self-worth and love. The parents' influence on the buyer's behaviour can be significant especially in those countries where they live with their grown-up children. The family of procreation consists of one's spouse and children who have a more direct influence on everyday buying behaviour [4].

In most Western societies three types of families dominate: the married couple, the nuclear family and the extended family. The married couple family consists of only the husband and the wife including the newly married couples or older couples who have already raised their children. The second type of family is known as the nuclear family which consists of the husband, wife and one or more children. The nuclear family along-with at least one grandparent living within the household is known as the extended family. Nowadays a fourth type of family is rising in number due to divorce, separation and out-of-wedlock births, which is known as the single parent family [5].

In India and in a few more countries, the joint family system was prevalent in earlier times where all the members of the family consisting of uncles, aunts, their children, grandparents and all others having a share in the property used to live together. This type of family is fast vanishing from India. As '*Business Today*' has reported that in today's scenario, the break up of the joint and extended family has a significant role to play in the emergence of new urban family as a customer.

According to it, in 1971 the average urban family consisted of 5.46 members, wherein individuals had little room for bonding. In 1997 there were only 4.6 members-a dimension that enables the members of a family to relate to one another and still have their own space [6]. Another survey done by the Operation Research Group called the Indian Readership Survey, 1995, covered both urban and rural India using a sample size of 165 million respondents. It was found that 74 percent of Indian households were nuclear and that the typical family across urban and rural India consisted of 3.9 individuals [7].

The family, as a unit, is an important consumer for many products, which are purchased for consumption by all family members. Thus, the same decision in many families may be made either by the husband or by the wife or both may have an equal voice. Children are also beginning to exert their influence on the family's purchase decisions. This is especially true in case of products such as television, stereo music systems, records and personal computers where the children are likely to have updated information about various brands and product attributes. Commenting on the consumer behaviour trends in the hi-fi stereo music today Vice President of Peico Electronics said, "It is the teenagers who select sets, and their papas just buy them" [8]. Definitions of some of the terms commonly used in family research are given in Table 1.1.

Functions of the Family

The functions of the family vary from culture to culture and also from one family form to the other. Basically the family performs four types of functions for its members i.e. providing financial support, emotional support, family lifestyle and socialisation.

Traditionally, the husband was responsible for providing the economic well being. But with the rise in working wives and teenage children doing part-time jobs, the economic role has changed. Family provides emotional support and assists its members to cope with personal and social problems. Family also establishes a suitable lifestyle for its members determining the importance to be placed on education, career, reading, selection of entertainment and recreational activities and dressing up etc. which influences their consumption pattern. Moreover, family helps in socialising its members, imparting to children and other members the basic values and modes of behaviour consistent with the culture [9].

Table 1.1: Common Terms Used in Family Research

Term	Definition
Household	All persons who occupy a housing unit: people living alone, a group of unrelated people, or a family.
Family	A group of two or more persons related by blood, marriage, or adoption, and residing together.
Nuclear Family	A group of two or more persons related to one another by blood, marriage, or adoption, and of the same or adjoining generations.
Extended Family	Family structures that extend beyond the nuclear family to include aunts, uncles, etc.
Family of Procreation	The family one establishes through marriage.
Family of Orientation	The family one is born into.

Source: Michael P. Heffring, "Measuring Family Decision-Making: Problems and Prospects", *Advances in Consumer Research*, Vol. 7 (1980), pp. 492-498.

How Families Make Purchase Decisions

One of the most important areas for marketers to understand in planning their strategies is how families reach their purchase decisions. Following are the major characteristics of a family: -

1. *A family makes, and spends money continuously for many years:* The sheer number of decisions is so large that it is almost impossible to measure them all or to generalise about them accurately.

2. *Family decisions are made with a private, intimate, social group:* They are therefore not easy to observe and may depend upon past personal histories within the family, which the researcher is unaware of.

3. *Family consumption decisions are often not independent from one another:* They are difficult to study in isolation. In most families, the family member's needs and desires for purchases exceed the limited income. The allocation of resources is thus necessary and trade-offs occur among alternative products and services.

4. *Family has multiple decision makers:* Decisions range from individual choices made by members within the home, to truly joint decisions that may involve any combination of members. The husband and wife might decide about buying a bed, while the wife and daughter might think of a dress. Capturing what actually goes on when multiple decision-makers are involved, is another area worthy of research.

5. *Family decision-making differs by the type of product being studied:* Most marketers are interested in family decision processes for "their" particular product or service.

6. *Families differ significantly among themselves:* Families differ in terms of individual personalities, wealth, age, social standing, lifestyles, goods already owned etc. In addition, decision styles also vary. Some families are

patriarchies, in which the father exercises influence over major consumer decisions, while others are matriarchies, in which the mother rules supreme; still others are egalitarian where the power is more equally shared, with the children perhaps weighing in with considerable influences of their own. Further, within each family, the styles may shift over time, as the spouse's work, and situations change, the children mature, and divorce may intervene [10].

Family. Decision-making

Family decision-making basically refers to the manner in which family members interact and influence each other when making purchase choices for the household [11]. Although a family is being recognised as the basic decision-making unit, marketers most frequently examine the attitudes and behaviour of one family member whom they believe to be the major decision-maker. To fully understand family decision-making, marketers need to identify which family members take on what roles [12].

Family Roles

There are multiple roles enacted within a household's buying process. Some roles are more important than the others depending on the product and situation. Also, it is possible for the same person to play all the roles or for many members to be involved at various stages [13]. Five of the most important buying roles identified by Kotler are:

Initiator: A person who first suggests the idea of buying the particular product or service.

Influencer: A person whose views or advice carries some weight in making the final decision.

Decider: A person who decides on any component of a buying decision: whether to buy, what to buy, how to buy, or where to buy.

Buyer: The person who makes the actual purchase.

User: A person who consumes or uses the product or service.

Seven of the most important buying roles enlisted by Wilkies are as follows [14]:

Stimulator: This person first brings up the idea of the purchase.

Influentials: These are the members whose opinions have either direct or indirect influences on the final purchase decision.

Experts: These members contribute information about the product, the possible options, where it can be bought and so on. Often, this person or persons will shop around, talk to friends or consult consumer reports to obtain the information that will be passed on to the other members.

Decision-maker: In a joint decision, several persons will perform in this role, which involves a decision about exactly what to buy or not to buy. In other purchases only one of the members will actually make the final decision, usually in the store.

Buyer: This person actually purchases the product, pays for it, and either takes it home or arranges for delivery. At times, this person is acting as the decision-maker and at times, as a purchasing agent for another person.

Consumer: This is the person who actually uses the product.

Caretaker: This is the person or persons who undertakes various tasks to store the product, prepare it for use and maintain it in an operating condition.

These roles can be enacted either openly or through non-verbal means. Several roles lead to gatekeeper activity. This means that a person can decide either to "let in" certain information or products if he or she is in control of the "gate" through which it would enter.

Schiffman and Kanuk have proposed eight distinct roles in the family decision-making process, which are as follows [15]:

Influencers: The family members who provide information to other members
about a product or service.

Gatekeepers: Those who control the flow of information about a product or service into the family.

Deciders: The member who makes the decision to buy or use the product or select the brand.

Buyers: Those who make the actual purchase.

Preparers: Those who make the product ready for consumption or use.

Users: Those who use or consume the product.

Maintainers: The member who repairs or maintains the product to keep it working.

Disposers: Family members who initiate or carry out the disposal or discontinuance of a particular product or service.

These roles show that different family members may be involved in different aspects of the purchase decision process and in consumption of the product or service that is bought. Each family member and his or her roles and behaviour are part of the social environment for the other family members [16]. Thus, family decision-making involves a study of the social interaction between family members and the resulting patterns of their reciprocal influence.

Dynamics of Husband-wife Decision-making

Marketers are interested in the relative amount of influence that a husband and a wife have on family consumption choices. Most surveys of family purchase influence have classified purchases as being husband-dominant, wife-dominant, joint (i.e., equal or syncratic) and autonomic (i.e., solitary or unilateral) [17].

When either partner is dominant for a particular product, that product decision is attributed to role specialisation [18]. Family members tend to specialise in products for which they have a particular interest. However the influence of various members differs depending on the stage of the decision-making process.

The husband-wife influence in family decisions depends on the specific product or service, the family role structure orientation and the specific stage in the decision-making process. These factors are also influenced by changing lifestyles, particularly the changes in the family lifestyle options associated with women working outside and the increased occurrence of dual income household [19].

Joint Decision and Role Conflict

The two basic conditions when families make a joint decision can occur are: either everyone agrees about the goals or they do not. This leads to two types of joint decisions: consensual and accommodative [20]. In a consensual decision, the goals are agreed upon. In the case of an accommodative decision, however, differences occur in the goals. Some of the decision strategies under goal consensus are [21]:

Role structure strategy: Here one member can simply assume the role of a specialist and handle most decisions on a routine basis.

Rule strategy: This strategy can be set up by members and someone can act as a controller to see that the rules are followed.

Problem-solving strategy: This strategy can be implemented by the use of an expert who can be relied on for good advice or family discussions can be held to discover a better solution. Also, multiple purchases sometimes help in solving particular issues.

When more than one person in a family is involved in making a purchase decision, some degree of conflict is likely [22]. Decision conflict arises when family members disagree about some aspect of the purchase decision. The means-end chain model provides a useful framework for analysing decision conflict [23]. Differences in end goals often create major conflicts because very different choice alternatives are likely to lead to incompatible ends. Serious negotiations may be required to resolve the conflicts.

In other cases, family members might agree on the desired end goal, yet disagree about the best means to achieve it. Again some means of resolving conflict is necessary. When either the means or the end are in conflict, family members are likely to disagree about the choice criteria for evaluating the choice alternatives.

Some of the strategies to be used when goals conflict with each other are as follows [24]:

Persuasive strategy: In this strategy a member is led to take a decision that he had rather not take.

Bargaining strategy: This tries to create conditions under which the member will want to take the decision.

Consumer Socialisation of Children

Consumer socialisation is the process by which "young people acquire skills, knowledge and attitudes relevant to their functioning in the market place" [25]. While television has a persuasive influence on what children see and how they react to certain brands, "the family is instrumental in teaching young people the rational aspects of consumption, including basic consumer needs [26].

Parents try to teach or influence their children to be more effective consumers in the following ways [27]:

1. They teach price-quality relations to their children, including experiences with the use of money and ways to shop for quality products.
2. They teach their children how to be effective comparison shoppers and how to buy products on sale.
3. Parents influence children's brand preferences.
4. Parents influence children's ability to distinguish fact from exaggeration in advertising.

Methods of Socialisation

Children learn these various methods of purchase and consumption behaviour from their parents. One method they use is observation. Children watch and imitate parental behaviour because parents serve as role models. Another method of learning is through co-shopping with the parent. A third method of socialisation is through direct experience.

Family Life Cycle

Family is a dynamic entity. The composition of a family changes over time and with that the family needs, behaviour of its members and the decision-making process also change. The change in composition in family is known as "family life cycle" which is basically the progression of stages through which many families pass. There is, however, another framework called "consumer life cycle", which explains the stages a consumer passes through in life reflecting the systematic effects of age, marital status, and the presence of children [28]. Schiffman and Kanuk have proposed the family life cycle model consisting of five stages. In this the general progression of an adult is considered over the period in question. These stages are [29]:

Stage 1: **Bachelorhood** - This stage consists of a young adult living apart from parents.

Stage 2: **Honeymooners** - It consists of a young married couple with no children.

Stage 3: **Parenthood** - This stage consists of a married couple with at least one child living at home.

Stage 4: **Post-parenthood** - This stage consists of an older married couple with no children living at home.

Stage 5: **Dissolution** - This consists of only one surviving spouse.

Wells and Guber have proposed the following eight-stage framework for a consumer-oriented family life cycle [30]:

1. **Young Single**: Unmarried, under thirty-five. Characterised by below average income, high discretionary spending and considerable freedom.

2. **Newly married**: Young, married, no children. Characterised by good financial situation, creation of a new household, new obligations and activities.

3. **Full nest I**: Married, youngest child under 6. Characterised by arrival of children, parents' loss of freedoms, new focus on home, incurring financial debt.

4. **Full nest II**: Married, youngest child 6-12. Characterised by increase in freedom of parents, improvement in financial situation, continuing focus on home.

5. **Full nest III**: Married, youngest child in teens. Characterised by increase in freedom of parents,

improvement in income, but pressure on saving for college, focus moving outside of home.

6. Empty nest I: Married, children have left home. Characterised by increase in freedom of parents, improvement in finances (income up, spending down) focus shifting to outside of home and extended family.

7. Empty nest II: Married, retired from work, children have left home. Characterised by drop in income and possible stress on finances due to medical concerns, substantial freedoms, possible focus on extended family.

8. Solitary survivor: Widowed, retired from work, children have left home. Characterised by lower income, possible health and loneliness problems, substantial freedoms, and possible focus on extended family.

The special needs and desires of families at each stage of the family life cycle offer unique opportunities to the marketers of various goods and services. The marketers make use of the concept of family life cycle to identify the target markets and to forecast the demand for a particular product. Dynamic socio-demographic changes in society have resulted in many non-traditional stages that a family or non-family household might pass through (childless couples, couples marrying later in life, single parents, unmarried couples or single person households) [31].

Profile of the Selected Durable Products

The industrial production data for year 1999-2000 has shown that the fastest growing segment in that period was the consumer durable segment, with a nearly 18 percent increase [32].

The durable products chosen for the purpose of study are audio system, car, personal computer, refrigerator, television and washing machine. The market profile of these six durable products is given below:

Audio System Market

Size of the audio system market is estimated to be Rs. 9000 million (2000-2001) and is expected to grow at the rate of around 5 percent in the following year [33]. Major players in this market are Philips, Videocon, BPL, Aiwa and Sony.

Classification of Audio Systems

The audio system market is quite diverse in terms of the product segments and the features available. It can be classified as follows:

Radio: These are portable radio receivers capable of receiving audio signals of different frequencies. Most popular in this segment are the battery-operated transistors and are sold extensively in the rural markets. Although this market is on a decline, with the introduction of FM service in most cities some interest has been revived in this segment. *HPS System:* Popularly known as "Walkman", the portable stereo has a limited market. In addition to being a cassette player some variants have a radio receiver capable of receiving FM signals as well. Models with the recording facility have limited use. Portable personal stereos with CD players are also available in India now.

MRR System: Mono radio recorders are the two-in-ones with single speaker and have radio receiver and cassette player with recorder. These sets are usually the first cassette players for the youngsters. They have low sound output of less than 15 watts and available in attractive colours and shapes.

SRR System: Stereo radio recorders are again portable two-in-one but with stereo sound output of medium level ranging between 20-120 watts. Available in different shapes and sizes, this segment has a very wide range of models. CD systems are available in the upper end of the spectrum.

Hi-Fi System: High fidelity audio systems are characterised by high sound output levels and are invariably three-in-ones with the CD player, cassette player (and recorder) and radio receiver. Remote control operated, it can be a multiple CD changer. A hi-fi audio system capable of playing video CDs as well are now readily available.

Trends in the Audio System Market

The important characteristics of the audio system market being observed in recent times are discussed in the following matter.

The need for general music being taken care of by TV, music systems is becoming the preserve of devoted niche preference listeners. Some analysts feel that most marketers are concentrating so much on the TV segment and are neglecting the audio systems. According to Sujata Rakhra, Vice President, ORG-MARG, "In the audio system the marketers have not been able to give many convincing **reasons to buy** to the consumer. Most advertisements, even when they go beyond showcasing products and talking about features, assume an audience of music lovers. Software and hardware marketers should align their forces to generate greater aggregate desire for music".

TV serves the purpose of incidental listening and music systems are becoming the preserve of niche listeners devoted to a highly individualised kind of music. The market for plain radios, though vast, has been declining. The reason behind this is that the penetration of all these products is high and the interest to replace it is very low. Except in rural India, the radio is no longer the reference point in a household for information and entertainment. Mono-tape players are dying out and stereo systems sound much better and don't cost so much more.

The urban market for audio equipment has declined. Most marketers are concerned about the urban market where almost all the stereo two-in-ones, compact discs (CD) players, personal stereos, car audio system, midis, minis and hi-fi systems sell.

According to N. Gupta, Videocon, "Sixty percent of the market is made up of low priced system-below Rs.4,000" [34]. There is an emergence and assertiveness of the new generation gives audio marketers some optimism. It is on the new crowd's demand that music systems are losing their tag as a "family purchase". The current urban young generation is aggressive in its wants and demands and wants a system in their own bedrooms. Moreover, the factor that makes a difference is the physical product styling. Technological advancement plays a major role in the audio market.

The CD player, which was considered a fancy possession some times ago, is within the reach of buyers with budgets not more than Rs.5,000. According to Harish Dayani, "In a country of 950 million there are only four lakhs CD players. While 275 million cassettes sell in a year, only four million CD's have been sold". The reason behind this is that the CD's are priced rather high for people to think buying too many of them. One way to tackle this is to ensure that the mass market gets a taste of digital sound quality. This can only be done by launching CD's at throw-away prices and by giving free samples.

In the audio market, where price is a stumbling block, multinationals are moving down the price scale. The unorganised sector is struggling to hold its own against the onslaught of the recent technological advances. Companies such as Sony, Panasonic, LG and Akai are aware that the big money will eventually come from people who move up the ladder as India's GDP grows.

Car Market

After a 60 percent growth in 1999-2000 over the previous year, the current year (2000-2001) is expected to see a lower growth of 12 to 15 percent on a much-expanded base of car sales [35]. The car market is clearly maturing with a full range of cars from Segment A economy models to the highest end segment E cars. This ensures that there is a car for every need. Players in car market are Maruti, Hyundai, Daewoo, Honda, General Motors, Ford, Fiat, Toyota and Tata.

Trends in the Car Market

In India, now novelty is no more a key driver for car sales and customers are more demanding and discerning now [36]. Cars are more affordable and available than they were before, thus serving to broad base the market. Additionally, increased options in used cars that are much more affordable and easily available have also led to increase in first time car buyers entering the market. Overall, the car market is very healthy.

The car market is led by Maruti with sale of Rs. 96,730 million (1999-2000) and a share of more than 50 percent of the market [37].The current trends in sales of Maruti cars across product segments are very strong and promising with a healthy growth in 1999-2000 over the previous year's sales [38]. Maruti offers life stage car options with a car for every segment of the car market in India.

Many auto giants that launched new products in this segment are trying to make changes in their strategies. Ford

India has projected demand for mid-size cars at 80,000 this year, which amounts to about 30 percent increase.

Huyndai has also been balancing its Santro and Accent within the existing capacity constraint and is looking for respite through operating a third shift. In a couple of months Huyndai expects to sell beyond the break-even of 70,000 cars and Ratan Tata has indicated that the Indica project would reach the level this fiscal year. Daewoo and Honda expect to get closer this year, achieving break-even in 2001-02 [39].

During 1999-2000 the passenger car industry crossed the 6,00,000 units mark. Passenger car sales during the financial year 1999-2000 increased to 6,39,000 units as compared to 410,000 units in the previous year. According to Society of Indian Automobiles Manufacturers, Maruti Udyog registered a 21.8 percent growth at 3.98 lakh cars but its market share dipped sharply to 62.2 percent during the year compared to 80 percent in 1998-99 [40]. Global leaders such as General Motors and Mercedes Benz recorded negative sales during the reviewed period. Multi-utility vehicles registered a 10.5 percent increase in sales at 1.23 lakh during 1999-2000 as compared to 1.11 lakh recorded in the previous year [41].

Personal Computer Market

Total personal computer (PC) sale in India crossed a million mark (1,125,235 units) during the year 1999-2000 [42]. The internet drove PC market in the second half of the last fiscal year (1999-2000). With more and more towns getting access to the net sale of PCs grew in B and C class cities. Fifty percent of the PC market is estimated to be held by the unorganised sector (assemblers). Top ten branded PC manufacturers account for around 45 percent of the market with the rest shared by regional players.

Trends in the PC Market

The PC market has two distinct customer segments viz. household and commercial/institutional. With the availability of the internet in most cities, the household segment is expanding fast.

So far, the infotech revolution seems to be changing things and 'computers for everybody' is an alluring vision for the new millennium. By one estimate, 70 percent of the world's installed PCs are connected in some way to some network [43]. Big time growth is expected in this segment once networking is regarded as a part of regular day-to-day functioning- like telephone conversations are today. With every year computer processing power going up involving smarter technologies and bigger economies of scale resulting in a fall in the computer price [44]. After liberalisation, in 1995-96, the Indian PC market grew 80 percent to reach 4.5 lakh units [45].

The largest home PC market in the Asia Pacific region is India. In most other markets PCs are mainly a corporate purchase, and are associated mainly with work. In India, however more than 50 percent of all PCs lie in the home segment. But most of this (65 percent) is with local manufacturers and assemblers who sell their machines below Rs. 40,000. In the consumer segment some analysts feel that the consumer is willing to pay a premium of 15 percent just for the quality that he is assured of in a brand. The household market buys PCs primarily for educational purposes (63 percent), carrying work home (49 percent) and internet usage (25 percent) [46]. The potential in the home segment, though, remains largely untapped, since the fear of technological obsolescence and expectation of still lower prices has led to many deferred purchases.

Brand Power in the PC Market: Brands are under pressure to show their worth. At one level, Indian players who had teamed up with foreign companies have now decided to sell their own labels. The HCL-HP marriage has fallen apart; though it sells Packard Bell in the home segment, it's busy pushing its own sub-brands, Busybee, Infiniti and Beanstalk. PCL no longer sells Dell. Wipro-Acer, though still selling Acer, has brought back its own Super Genius from the cold storage. The allure of the foreign brand, unless marketed by the company itself, has worn thin.

At the upper-end, things are different. Foreign brands do command a degree of prestige, and so do the home-grown brands that hope to emulate them (such as HCL's Infiniti and Wipro's Super Genius). These marketers poise as guardians of the infotech needs of a wide base of large, regular clients. Since business-to-business bulk deals are often struck on a world-wide basis, brands such as Compaq and IBM start with a big advantage with MNCs.

In any product, distribution makes a huge difference. HCL, India's top PC marketer, claims a presence in 300 cities. Typically big brands operate by sending their teams across to big companies to strike direct deals and to look after all their infotech needs. Thus, spreading out is one aspect used by big companies and providing intelligent service is another. In fact, Vintron's claimed ground-level advantage suggests that even middle and lower zone buyers are looking for solutions. In response, local distributors and dealers are calling themselves infotech consultants and even providing tele-support and sending technicians down when a problem erupts. In order to stay ahead marketers are offering 'solutions'. This involves creating a buffer of support services and software solutions around the system. The solutions-approach means that marketers are tailoring products to suit specific needs, thus doing the ultimate form of segmentation: treating each buyer differently. Besides, marketer's experience teaches them to anticipate what a customer would want. Marketers have a good impression of how a big company would want its PCs configured and how a smaller one would.

Meanwhile, the home PC revolution is forcing marketers to be more sensitive to the individual buyer. Research companies are already talking of a segmentation format based on the individual's motivations and relationship with technology. India is still a laggard by global standards. Even when income-per-head figures rise, English not widely understood poses a problem. Thus, what is required is a Hindi graphic user interface.

Trends in the technological specifications: Several changes took place on the technology front which are responsible for the shape that the market has taken. Since March 2000, the clock speeds have nearly doubled with AMD machines with 1 gigahertz processors making an entry. The advent of the Intel 810 chipset based motherboards with their built-in audio and video cards helped bring price-points down, not only in the entry-level segment, but also in the higher end of the market. The hard disc capacities moved up from 2 GB to 4 GB to 8 GB during the year even when the price points remained constant or came down. Minimum RAM also moved up from 32 MB to 64 MB, and for home systems even touched 128 MB. PC peripherals also proliferated, thereby also contributing to higher unit values, particularly in the home segment.

Popular add-ons included web cams, CD writers, and digital versatile disk drives (DVDs).

Refrigerator Market

Refrigerator market size is estimated to be 2.4 million units (2000-2001). Of this, whereas the frost free refrigerator segment has de-grown by 6.9 percent, the direct cool refrigerator segment has de-grown by 3.4 percent over the previous year [47]. At 0.34 millions units, frost free refrigerators accounted for 14.5 percent of total refrigerator sales in the year 2000-2001. Major players in the Indian refrigerator market are Whirlpool, Kelvinator, Godrej, Videocon, BPL, LG and Samsung.

Classification of the Refrigerator Market

The refrigerator market can be broadly divided in two segments viz. frost free refrigerators and direct cool refrigerators [48].

Frost Free Refrigerators: In most western countries frost-free technology is used for the household refrigerators. Based on the principle of forced convection, they are different from the conventional direct cool refrigerators in the sense that the evaporator (cooling coil) is located outside the refrigerated compartments. Air as cooling medium is forced over the evaporator by the help of a blower that then circulates in the refrigerated area. Different temperatures are maintained in different compartments of the refrigerator by regulating the quantity of air allowed in the compartment. A major advantage of these refrigerators is a frost-free interior and multiple compartments at different temperatures. Frost-free refrigerators can be placed in four groups according to the size viz. less than 225 litre, 225-270 litre, 271-310 litre and more than 310 litre. Smaller refrigerators (< 270 litre) account for around 70 percent of total sales.

Direct Cool Refrigerators: The evaporator or the freezer in this case is located inside the refrigerator compartment and cooling takes place because of natural convection. Despite of inherent technological disadvantages, refrigerators based on this technology are the most popular in the Indian market and account for 85 percent of total refrigerator sales. Main reason for their popularity, apart from lower price, is the perception that ice formation around the freezer helps preserve the food during frequent power cuts.

According to the size, direct cool refrigerators can be further classified into three groups viz. less than 185 litre, 185-225 litre and more than 225 litre Smaller refrigerators (< 185 litre) account for 75 percent of total sales.

Trends in the Refrigerator Market

Real value of refrigeration for food preservation is not much of a felt need of Indian people who eat freshly cooked food at every meal, and that too without any packaged inputs whatsoever. In that sense market's evolution remains tied to Indian eating habits. In the US, where frozen foods occupy huge amounts of space, frost-free refrigerators are quite popular. But in India, things are different. Firstly, the freezer unit is almost ignored in the purchase decision (ice making being its only function). Moreover, vegetarian and non-vegetarian households differ substantially in their food storage requirements [49].

A survey made by ORG-GFK found that refrigerators are all set to emerge number one in the hierarchy of consumer durables purchased in the country. In fact, market experts are now predicting a boom in refrigerator sales in the next few years. According to Ms Sujata Rakra, the managing director of ORG-GFK, the extreme high growth recorded for CTV sales is now tapering off [50].

It has been found by ORG-GFK that the market penetration of coloured televisions has been fairly good which is leading its way for a boom in refrigerators sales in the coming years.

Companies today are trying to make products affordable to practically every household whatever the income level. Companies in the refrigerator segment are trying to play the price point game. In the refrigerator segment radical cost reengineering is not possible, but companies in this segment are moving downscale, and are making fridge for under Rs 7,000 since the major business for companies comes from the low-priced zones [51]. Price is an important criterion in rural markets and companies such as Godrej-GE is trying to boost sales through consumer financing schemes in conjunction with Countrywide Finance. Thus, companies are trying to come out with products that are affordable, consumer-friendly and aimed at semi-urban and rural India.

Colour Television Market

Colour television market (CTV) market in India is estimated to be around 5 million units (2000-2001) having shown a marginal growth of around 5 percent. Year 2000-2001 saw a slowdown in the CTV market and the growth was far below 20 percent that the previous year experienced [52]. Major players in the Indian CTV market are BPL, Videocon, Onida, Aiwa, Samsung, LG, Sony and Panasonic. At the same time there are Chinese brands who have aggressive plans for the Indian market viz. Konka and TCL. In addition to these brands, this year saw the resurgence of several regional players like Texla, Salora, Rangs, Oscar and

Futec who offered CTVs at much lower than the ruling prices of larger brands.

Classification of the CTV Market

CTV market can be classified on the basis of screen sizes. CTVs are available in five major screen sizes viz. 14, 20, 21, 25 and 29 inches although larger and smaller sized TVs are also available but form a very small part. Apart from the screen size, CTVs can be further classified on the basis of the features available that govern their position in the price spectrum in a size category. These features include the sound output, number of channels available, multi-lingual menus, automatic picture control mechanism etc. Flat screen variants in different screen sizes are also available now. Price of colour TVs range from Rs.6000-35,000 in general depending upon the screen size (14-29 inches) and the features, although larger sets are available at much higher prices.

Trends in the CTV Market:

In India, the coloured television market (CTV) has undergone three distinct phases. The sector reached the growth path in the 1982-89 period, when the government gave up its socialist approach and embraced consumerism for the first time. Many companies such as Weston, Crown, Televista, Dyanora entered this sector. The profitability of the venture encouraged the State governments to enter the TV sector which lead to joint ventures such as Uptron and Keltron.

TV was a highly profitable business in 1989. There were around 150 companies in the introduction stage of the PLC when about 1.3 million CTVs and about 4 million black and white TVs were sold.

After that, fiscal crisis hit in the early 1990's. Excise rates duty went up, the rupee came down and there was a slump in the industry. Between 1989-93 sales stagnated and the CTV industry saw its first phase of consolidation. Many companies got wiped out and the period saw the clear emergence of market leaders such as BPL, Videocon and Mirc Electronic's Onida. These companies shared about 50 percent of the CTV business between themselves.

The competitive scenario changed in the 1994-99 period with the gradual entry of MNCs, the Koreans and the Japanese. Now, most international brands have local operations. Fierce price competition and innovative marketing strategies like 'buy a TV for a rupee' and 'bring in the old and take home the new' from Akai have changed the market place radically. Akai, marketed by Baron Electronics, compounded these tactics with direct price wars, which lead to a 50 percent drop in prices from the levels of the mid-90s.

The CTV industry is also one sector where the price wars have affected dealers. Margins in television retailing are probably the lowest for any retail product and dealers typically work on low inventories of about 15 days to maximise profitability. Therefore dealers sell at a discount and frequently under-cut each other.

In the second half of the 90s market expansion in this sector occurred because of the increased affordability of CTV's. During this period the CTV market experienced a compounded annual rate of growth of about 23 percent.

Indicative of a maturing market, the focus in the CTV business is slowly shifting from price to technology. The rate of product introduction has gone up and new models highlight enhanced product features and product styling to achieve product differentiation. LG's Golden Eye technology, Sony's Trinitron and Videocon's Bazooka have succeeded in expanding their market growth rate.

Some weaker firms have been reduced to the regional level. Others like, Salora have begun offering multinational companies their manufacturing facilities. Market leaders such as BPL, Videocon and Onida have protected their positions at the top despite end-product prices coming down. They have been able to improve their profitability measured in terms of their operating margins. Thus, these companies have shown that competition is not necessarily bad for producers.

Demand from those upgrading their preference is estimated at 40 percent of the total demand. The base of installed CTV's in India is estimated around 21 million of which 50 percent of the sets are more than 5 years old. Forty percent of the demand for CTV's in India is priced at less than Rs. 14000 amongst which 30 percent for less than Rs. 12,000. This segment is growing rapidly, as CTV's are becoming increasingly affordable for the majority of India's population [53].

With an increase in competition, a 21-inch CTV, which in 1994 was available for 21,500, is now being retailed at less than Rs.10,000. Thus, the consumer has benefited because of stiff competition and with the entry of foreign companies in this segment [54].

Washing Machine Market

Washing machine market in India is estimated to be around one million units in year 2000-2001. The market however experienced a de-growth of 8.5 percent over the previous year (1999-2000) [55]. Major players in the washing machine market are Videocon, Whirlpool, LG, BPL, Godrej, Electrolux and IFB.

Classification of the Washing Machine Market

Washing machines can be broadly classified as semi-automatic and fully automatic, depending upon the extent of programming of the wash cycle that can be done.

Semi-Automatic Washing Machines: These machines are invariably twin-tub; one tub meant for washing of clothes and the other for rinsing. The rinsing operation leaves the clothes in a semi dry state. Manual intervention is quite necessary in the complete wash cycle. They can be further classified on the basis of the capacity of the machine (in terms of the cloth weight) which are less than 3.5 kg, 3.5-5 kg and more than 5 kg. Machines with more than 5 kg capacity sold the most during the year (2000-2001), accounting for more than 50 percent of the total semi-automatic washing machine sale. This segment also showed a growth of 69 percent while the overall semi-automatic segment experienced a de-growth of 9.5 percent. Semi-automatic washing machines are priced between Rs.5000-9000 depending upon the size and features.

Fully Automatic Washing Machines: These machines are single tub machines with either pulsator, agitator or tumble-wash technology. Once the clothes are loaded and the washing cycle programmed, the clothes are finally ready in almost dry state. Manual intervention is not required once the wash cycle has been set. They can also be classified as either top-loading or front-loading. Where as IFB was the only manufacturer of front-loading washing machines in India till some time back, several other players are now offering them. Quite interestingly, front-loading segment showed a growth of 32 percent while the top-loading machine sale dropped by 19 percent during year 2000-2001. Price of the fully automatic washing machines ranges between Rs.11,000-25,000.

Trends in the Washing Machine Market

An in-house research survey by Godrej revealed that after refrigerators the two most important big-ticket household appliances in India are washing machines and cooking systems. Now companies are successfully moving towards mini-metros and small towns in selling the concept of washing machines. Companies such as Videocon who were selling their product in metros, mini-metros and A-class cities felt the need of washing machines in small towns. Through research they found out that small-scale sector players made a crude device which didn't do any effective washing, and people were being charged about Rs. 3,000 for it. In 1996, Videocon took its twin-tub machine did away with the rinser and drier functions, and turned it into a single-tub wash-only machine and priced it at Rs. 2,900. In small towns labour is in abundance and people have both the time and space for rinsing, wringing and pre-drying. To get away from the drudgery out of beating clothes with a wooden club is the benefit for which people are ready to pay [56].

At present, BPL is the largest player in consumer electronics and home appliances in India. In the car sector Maruti is the largest player. Unlike the pre-1991 players (in other markets) that weren't accustomed to foreign competition, there has been a lot of change since 1980s in India. Now companies have to match the global efficiency standards and have to be innovative to satisfy consumers.

Summary

The family, as a unit, is an important consumer for many products. The individual members' buying behaviour is influenced by the family in which he is born namely the family of orientation and the family consisting of its spouse and children, namely, family of procreation. Family provides its members with financial and emotional support, decides the lifestyle to be adopted and ensures an environment for socialisation. Purchase decision-making in a family is a complex process with members adopting different roles at different stages of the process. The process involves joint decision-making and conflict resolution in the family. Another factor affecting the decision-making process is its stage in the family life cycle. Over the period there has been a shift in the traditional roles with female members and children influencing family purchase decisions much more actively. Indian consumer durable market has also undergone several changes during past few years and is ever evolving. These products are at different stages of their life cycle and accordingly offer varied technology options to the customers.

Notes

1. Leon G. Schiffman and Leslie Lazar Kanuk, ***Consumer Behaviour***, 6th ed. (Prentice-Hall of India, New Delhi, 1997), p. 346.

2. Ingrid C. Kildegaard, "A Household is Not a Family", ***Journal of Advertising Research***, Vol. 7 (June 1967), pp. 44-46.

3. Peter J Paul and Olson C Jerry, ***Consumer Behaviour: Marketing Strategy Perspectives*** (Richard D. Irwin, Homewood, Ill., 1987), p. 447.

4. Philip Kotler, ***Marketing Management: Analysis, Planning, Implementation and Control***, 9th ed. (Prentice-Hall of India, New Delhi, 1996), p. 179.

5. Leon G. Schiffman and Leslie Lazar Kanuk, ***Consumer Behaviour***, 6th ed. (Prentice-Hall of India, New Delhi, 1997), p. 347.

6. Shailesh Dobhal, "Selling to the New Urban Family", ***Business Today***, February 22, 1999, pp. 66-81.

7. Polomy Dhawan, "Clues to Change: IRS 1995", ***Advertising and Marketing***, Vol. 15 (March 1996), pp. 24-31.

8. "Understanding Consumers", Marketing for Managers, **SOM, MS-6, IGNOU**.

9. Leon G. Schiffman and Leslie Lazar Kanuk, ***Consumer Behaviour***, 6th ed. (Prentice-Hall of India, New Delhi, 1997), pp. 347-348.

10. William L. Wilkie, ***Consumer Behaviour***, 3rd ed. (John Wiley and Sons, New York, 1994), pp. 399-400.

11. Peter J. Paul and Olson C. Jerry, ***Consumer Behaviour***, 3rd ed. (Richard D. Irwin, Homewood, Ill., 1993), pp. 515-516.

12. Raymond L. Horton, ***Buyer Behaviour: A Decision-Making Approach*** (Charles E Merrill Publishing Company, New York, 1984), pp.372-380.

13. John C.Mowen, ***Consumer Behaviour***, 3rd ed. (Macmillan Publishing Company, New York, 1993), pp.598-608.

14. William L. Wilkie, ***Consumer Behaviour***, 3rd ed. (John Wiley and Sons, New York, 1994), pp. 399-400.

15. Leon G. Schiffman and Leslie Lazar Kanuk, ***Consumer Behaviour***, 6th ed. (Prentice-Hall of India, New Delhi, 1997), pp. 353-354.

16. Del I. Hawkins, *et al*, ***Consumer Behaviour: Implications for Marketing Strategy***, 3rd ed.
(Business Publications, Texas, USA, 1986), pp. 276-284.

17. Kim P. Corfman, "Perceptions of Relative Influence: Formation and Measurement", ***Journal of Marketing_Research***, Vol. 28 (May 1991), pp. 125-136.

18. Harry L. Davis and Benny P. Regaux, "Perception of Marital Roles in Decision Processes", ***Journal of_Consumer Research***, Vol. 1 (June 1974), pp. 55-62.

19. Leon G. Schiffman and Leslie Lazar Kanuk, ***Consumer Behaviour***, 6th ed. (Prentice Hall of India, New Delhi, 1997), pp. 353-354.

20. Michael B. Menasco and David J. Curry, "Utility and Choice: An Empirical Study of Wife/Husband Decision-Making", ***Journal of Consumer Research***, Vol. 15 (March 1989), pp. 87-97.

21. Daniel Seymour and Greg Lessne, "Spousal Conflict Arousal: Scale Development", ***Journal of Consumer Research***, Vol. 11 (December 1989), pp. 810-820.

22. Alvin Burns and Donald Granbois, " Factors Moderating the Resolution of Preference Conflict in Family Automobile Purchasing", ***Journal of Marketing Research***, February 1977, pp. 68-77.

23. Peter J. Paul and Olson C. Jerry, ***Consumer Behaviour***, 3rd ed. (Richard D. Irwin, Homewood, Ill., 1993), pp. 519-520.

24. William L. Wilkie, ***Consumer Behaviour***, 3rd ed. (John Wiley and Sons, New York, 1994), pp. 403-404.

25. Henry Assael, ***Consumer Behaviour and Marketing Action***, 5th ed. (Kent Publishing Company, Boston, 1995), pp. 572-577.

26. George P. Moschis, "The Role of Family Communication in Consumer Socialisation of Children and Adolescents", ***Journal of Consumer Research***, Vol. 11 (March 1985), pp. 898-913.

27. Henry Assael, ***Consumer Behaviour and Marketing Action***, 5th ed. (Kent Publishing Company, Boston, 1995), pp. 572-577.

28. William L. Wilkie, ***Consumer Behaviour***, 3rd ed. (John Wiley and Sons, New York, 1994), pp. 403- 406.

29. Schiffman, Leon G and Kanuk, Leslie Lazar, ***Consumer Behaviour***, 6th ed. (Prentice Hall of India, New Delhi, 1997), pp. 360-366.

30. William D. Wells and George Guber, "Lifecycle Concept in Marketing Research", ***Journal of Marketing__Research***, Vol.3 (November 1966), pp. 355-363.

31. Murphy P. Patrick and Staples A. William, "A Modernised Family-Life-Cycle", ***Journal of Consumer_Research***, Vol. 6 (June 1979), pp. 12-22.

32. "The Insider", ***The Economic Times: Investor's Guide***, May 15, 2000, p. 8.

33. www.**etintelligence**.com/ETRB/reports.

34. Mitu Jayashankar, "Audio Products: A Survey", ***Advertising and Marketing***, November 1-15, 1997, pp. 54-58.

35. Sanjeev, Sharma, "Cars Are More Affordable Today", ***The Economic* Times,** May 29, 2000,
p. 8.

36. Indranil Ghosh, "Car Sales Cross Six Lakh Mark in 1999-2000", ***Business India***, May 1-14, 2000, p. 30.

37. Indranil Ghosh, "Uphill Tasks", ***Business India***, July 24 -August 6, 2000, pp. 78-80.

38. "Maruti Stays Ahead of the Car Race", ***The Hindustan Times***, June 3, 2000, p. 16.

39. Radhika Dhawan, "Driving Partner", ***Business World***, February 5, 2001, pp. 32-33.

40. Suveen K. Sinha, "Maruti in a Midnight Alley", ***Business Today***, February 6, 2001, pp. 46-48.

41. Kanwaldeep Singh, "Auto Sales to Move in Slow Gear", ***Sunday Times of India***, June 4, 2000, p. 16.

42. Krishna Kumar, "Industry Analysis: Desktops and Notebooks", ***Dataquest,*** July 15, 2000, pp. 140-154.

43. Raman Rakesh, "Prosperity Patterns", ***Advertising and Marketing***, February 1-15, 1997, pp. 38-43.

44. Raman Rakesh, "Computers for Free: Trends Personal Computers", ***Advertising and Marketing,*** December 31, 1996, pp. 106-107.

45. Raman Rakeh, "Addressal Systems: Trends PC", ***Advertising and Marketing***, February 16-28, 1997, pp. 56-57.

46. Roshin Poviah, "People and Products: Homing In", ***Advertising and Marketing***, May 31,1999, p. 14.

47. Manoj Narula, "Whirl of a Time", ***Business India***, May 15-28, 2000, pp. 88-90.

48. Roshun Povaiah, "Fresh Focus: A Cover Report on BPL", ***Advertising and Marketing***, September 30, 1999, pp. 35-41.

49. Aloknanda Chakraborty, "Springing Right Back: A Cover Report on Godrej GE", ***Advertising and Marketing,*** February 15, 1999, pp. 40-46.

50. Kala Vijayraghavan, "White Goods: Cool Fridges are Hottest", ***The Economic Times,*** June 12, 2000, p. 1.

51. Pritika Chopra, "Luck Lustre: A Cover Report on LG Electronics", ***Advertising and Marketing,*** March 31, 1999, pp. 42-47.

52. Shilpa Udeshi, "Tracking Competition: No More Picture Perfect Than This", ***The Economic Times,*** May 17, 2000, p. 8.

53. BPL ltd **Annual Report** 1998-99, pp. 40-41.

54. Vinod Mahanta, "Consumer Electronics: The Colour Fades", ***Business Today,*** December 6, 2000, p. 24.

55. Bhupesh Bhandari, "Videocon's Big Battle", ***Business World,*** August 16, 1999, pp. 30-32.

56. Bhanu Pande, "Spreading Wider: A Cover Report on Videocon", ***Advertising and Marketing***, July 31, 1998, pp. 48-53.

2

Studies on Family Purchases: Global and the Indian Experience

This chapter presents a review of the existing literature in order to gain insights into the research work undertaken in this area. The review of literature has resulted in classification of the research work conducted in this area into four sections. Section I contains studies with the exploration of product category differences, their relationship to family decision-making and the structure of husband and wife roles. Section II covers studies relating to investigation of the determinants of joint decision-making when goals conflict with each other. In Section III, the studies pertaining to the changing role of women and children are reviewed. In Section IV, the studies that have been conducted in India are taken up. Although related to the topics covered in above sections, these studies put the Indian families into perspective.

I

Studies on Exploration of Product Categories and Family Decision-making

The following are the major studies, which deal with the exploration of product category differences, their relationship to family decision-making and the structure of husband and wife roles.

Wolgast's Study

Wolgast studied the role played by husbands and wives in making a purchase decision. Her study was based on a cross-section of families in all parts of the USA. Most of the data was from a panel study using multi-stage area sampling, initiated in June 1954, by the Survey Research Centre of the University of Michigan and sustained over a period of two-and-a-half years [1]. Interviews were obtained alternatively with heads of a family i.e., either husband or wife. The respondents were selected by random methods in each family.

In this study, decisions with regard to saving and handling family expenses, buying household goods such as furniture, appliances, or other big items for the house, buying a car and handling family expenses were considered. The role husbands and wives play in decision-making was tested through the following hypotheses: (1) How do husbands and wives describe their respective roles in some of the major kinds of economic decision-making? (2) Do the wishes and buying plans expressed by the husband show any difference from those expressed by the wife and if so, what kind of differences exist? (3) Is there any difference in the rate of fulfillment of buying plans expressed by the husband and the wife?

Implications of the study: In the American family, economic decisions are most commonly made jointly by husbands and wives. There is no support in the data for the notion that the economic affairs of an American family are primarily the province of the husband. Both the husband and the wife most frequently report that each of the functions, "handling the money and the bills" and "seeing to it that some money gets saved", is a joint endeavour. Where this is not so, the wife is somewhat more likely than the husband to assume the major role.

At the same time, there seems to be an implicit division of responsibility, growing more pronounced with increasing age and the length of marriage. For example, the husband takes a major role in planning car purchases, and the wife in planning home-appliance purchases [2].

Regarding expressed buying plans, husbands and wives show very similar frequencies of plans, though durable household goods are often mentioned as "wife's plans" and automobiles as "husband's plans". This similarity speaks for general agreement between the husband and the wife about the family plans. Apparently most of the buying intentions expressed in response to survey questions have already been discussed in the family. The plans and wishes of a spouse are generally known and readily elicited. This is true for the husband and the wife respondents.

Viewing greater influence by the wife as a possibility, there are two other explanations: (1) "Handling" the money and the bills is often the duty of the wife. Perhaps the wife is closer to the family budget and able to plan more realistically. (2) It is possible that men and women react somewhat differently to the interviewing situation. The wife may state the family's plans cautiously, trying to predict the family purchases. The husband, on the other hand, may have a greater tendency to express his hopes and wishes.

Either of these two possibilities, or both together, would account for the small but consistent difference in fulfillment rates. Both are consistent with the conclusion that economic decisions are made in a democratic fashion in American families.

The results also indicate that, in consumer surveys concerned with a broad range of expenditures, the husband and the wife are equally desirable respondents. If reactions are sought to various specific features of automobiles, or preferences for one type of car over another, the husband might make better respondents.

Conversely, wives might be preferred for a detailed study of household goods. Where plans to purchase are used as a tool in forecasting, samples of the husband and those of the wife would yield similar results. However, taking plans just in relation to fulfillment, wives are slightly more accurate respondents.

Webster's Study

In a study conducted by Webster in (1994), the following conclusions were drawn with regard to the traditional role specialisation and purchase behaviour:

1. Traditional role specialisation affects, which spouse has dominance with respect to specific products. For example, the husband dominated in purchase decisions for such product categories as insurance, automobiles and televisions. On the other hand, the wife dominated in purchase decisions for products associated with the homemaker role, such as appliances, groceries and washing machines. The relative influence on a purchase decision is higher for a spouse who is highly involved in the purchase and desires that reflect his or her individual interests and preferences.

2. Traditional role specialisation influences the relative dominance with respect to product attributes. Within the family, men have traditionally been task-oriented leaders, while women have led in social and emotional behaviour. Therefore, in purchasing decisions, the husband tends to concern themselves with relatively important and functional product attribute, e.g., price, while the wives concentrates on relatively minor aesthetics. Traditional role specialisation affects relative influence on or during decision phases. Traditionally, the husband dominated in the important decision phases (i.e., decision to buy), whereas the wife

dominated in the minor phases (i.e. suggesting the purchase) [3].

Quall's Study

This study examines the impact of sex role orientation on the outcome of a family decision to purchase a house. A relatively strong relationship is found between sex role orientation and the degree of household influence, preference agreement, mode of conflict resolution and decision outcome. Finally, it was found that the household decision behaviour can better be explained in the context of a theoretical network of household relationships rather than through a series of bivariate family relationships. Quall asserted that the sex role preferences reflect the societal standards and a perception of these sex roles affects the decision-making process [4].

Komarovsky's Study

Komarovsky indicated that joint involvement in decision-making is found to occur most in middle-income families and among younger couples and is related to the extent of husband-wife communication. Apparently among older couples role specialisation becomes more rigid [5]. Taking a somewhat different approach he advanced the idea based on the examination of various empirical studies, that there is greater autonomy with regard to expenditures at the bottom and at the top of the socio-economic hierarchy than among the middle classes. The studies she examined support the fact that the wife in the lower socio-economic classes seems to have greater influence in decision-making relating to expenditures. In addition, in all social classes she found a higher rate of joint decision-making on spending among young couples.

Study by Davis and Ragsdale's

In this study an attempt has been made to predict the preferences of husband and wife. This study proposes an anchoring process where an attempt is being made to adjust for the ways in which we are likely to differ from others. In five experiments, 220 husbands and wives predicted the preferences of their spouses for 20 new product concepts. Both husbands and wives anchored heavily on their preferences. Moreover, they consistently adjusted for beliefs about the relative influence that their spouses would have on the purchase decision for each of the concepts. On an average, people are not accurate in predicting spousal preferences. Almost half of the people would have been more accurate by simply reporting their own preferences. Most of the subjects had difficulty in isolating systematic adjustment factors that were more diagnostic of spousal preferences than their own preferences [6].

Study by Sharp and Mott

The findings question many of the traditional beliefs regarding the intra-familial assignment of consumer decision-making roles. There is little evidence that in a larger number of Detroit families, one or the other spouse makes all the decisions with regard to car, life insurance, food, apartment, vacation, money and bills. For example, while the husbands usually select which car to buy, they generally do not make the final decision with regard to food expenditures. Also, in selecting a new home and deciding where to go on vacaticns, married couples rely largely on consensus rather than on unilateral decision-making.

Except in case of life insurance, the age of the wife is not associated in any manner with variations in decision patterns in her family. It was found that the husband exerts more influence than the wife in the purchase of automobiles, less influence than the wife in deciding how much to spend on food, and equal influence in deciding about vacations and housing. Income differences between urban households was found to be closely related to patterns of decision-making which are consistent with the additional knowledge of the characteristics of high and low-income families [7].

Study by Ferber and Lee

In this study, the influence of husband-wife in family purchase behaviour is being studied. Using the concept of a family financial officer (FFO), the family is found to be not homogenous in its financial and purchase behaviour. Further it was found that if the husband is the FFO, the couple is more likely to save a higher proportion of income and would purchase automobiles less frequently [8].

Ferber's Study

Ferber has developed a simplified decision-making framework wherein specific attention is given to family saving and spending. Ferber has divided the family's economic decision into two types-financial and non-financial. The decisions in financial grouping include decisions dealing with money management, savings, spending and asset management. All other decisions that a family may make are grouped together under non-financial. It may be noted that in Ferber's framework both financial and non-financial decisions are affected by the available financial resources of the family, by the objectives or goals of the family and by the attitudes of the family members.

The above framework takes into consideration the fact that family decisions in some cases are dominated by influences that are external and not under the family's control. In particular these include economic and political events in the community in which the family lives and personal experiences of the individual family members such as births, deaths, marriage and accidents [9].

Ferber's investigation combined observational techniques and those of sample surveys. He interviewed each member in a sampled family first in the absence of other members, and then in their presence. Therefore, he was able to check one member's responses against others, and to observe the behaviour of the family as a whole. Discrepancies in the answers of husbands and wives made it possible to find a typical pattern of decision-making [10].

Hempel's Study

This study highlights cross-cultural comparison of husband-wife interaction in specific house-buying [11]. The findings indicate that perceived roles vary more by sex of the respondent and the relevant stage in the decision process than by the cultural context of the purchase. According to him the husband-wife agreement in both the cultures is related to family size, the stage in life cycle, attitudes toward previous residence and life-style (particularly physical mobility). Thus, role structure in household decision behaviour is partially determined by education, occupational prestige and wife's employment.

Study by Blood and Wolfe

Blood and Wolfe focused on examining bivariate relationships involving the decision role structure of the household.The major findings of this study were:

1. Husband dominance in household decision-making is directly related to cultural norms of the society.

2. The power to make household decisions is related to the resources husbands and wives bring to the household.

3. The husband's influence in household decision behaviour is directly related to his income, education and occupation.

Blood and Wolfe justify the use of wives as sole respondents by the fact that husbands and wives usually agree sufficiently to make it possible to rely on one partner's responses [12].

Study by Cunningham and Green

The trend towards sex role egalitarianism in household purchasing roles is related to the increase in joint decision behaviour. This study is concerned with changes that have occured over the past eighteen years in the roles of the husband and the wife in family purchase decision-making. The most dramatic change in decision roles found in the study occurred with respect to automobiles. Here the data indicate that a basic change in market composition has occurred. Formerly a male dominated product, automobile purchase appears to be increasingly becoming a joint decision in the family.

The major implication that these findings offer to marketing management is that it is difficult to generalise the impact that changes in the environment will have on family purchasing patterns. While family decision-making roles have been changing in response to environmental change, all products apparently have not been affected in the same way [13].

Studies on Money-Management

Of the three studies that provided information on money management in urban areas, two were conducted by the survey research centre of the university of Michigan and yielded similar results [14]. The studies revealed that the wife shouldered the responsibility of money management most of the time, but in a substantial number of families, the responsibility was either shared or looked after by the husband. Sharp and Mott also noted that the husband is likely to shoulder this responsibility more often and the wife less often among higher-income families 15]. The Peoria-Decatur panel of young married couples, suggested that the husband generally carry a larger share of this burden than the wife. Whether this difference is due to the nature of the sample, location, or different time period cannot be ascertained [16].

Zober's research work deals with the determinants of husband-wife buying roles [17]. P D Converse found that the gender of the purchaser depends on the economic bracket in which the family falls and also whether the family is a rural or urban one [18]. An experiment explaining the role of the husband and wife in decision-making was conducted at Iowa State University. The object of this experiment was to ascertain how much influence each spouse had in the decision-making process and to learn whether each could predict his or her actions. An analysis of the influence was restricted to three variables. The study disclosed that the husband did most of the talking and had the greatest influence on the decision. The wife was the peacemaker. Decision-making varies from item to item and for certain items, more planning is necessary. In shopping for major products such as appliances or automobiles, the wife rarely acts alone. These products are purchased jointly. In another research it was stated that the amount of cooperation between husband and wife is also an outgrowth of social and economic status. Among lower-income families, the purchase of an automobile is a combined decision, whereas the upper-class husband makes the decision alone. Yet this is not necessarily the pattern for other economic decisions. The conflicting values of the husband and the wife also influence the purchase decision.

Wilkie's Study

An example of process methodology was provided by Wilkies, who measured family influence in four stages: problem recognition, search, alternative evaluation (intention) and purchase or choice. His decision-process measures the following [19]:

1. Who was responsible for the initial problem recognition?
2. Who was responsible for acquiring information about the purchase alternatives?
3. Who made the final decision as to which alternative should be purchased?
4. Who made the actual purchase of the product?

The research using this methodology produced better results than more global measures of influence. Additionally, the husband and the wife within families were found to hold similar perceptions about their relative influence for a given phase of the decision process.

Davis' Study

Davis carried out the most thorough study of marital roles among 100 families living in four Chicago suburbs. Couples were asked a series of questions about the relative influence of husband and wife on the purchase of two durable goods-an automobile and living room furniture. A comparison of these two views reveals considerable variability in the husband-wife roles. It is also interesting to note that the perception of the wife and the perception of the husband differ as to who has the greater influence [20].

Study by Shuptrine and Samuelson

In this study a partial replication of Davis' work done in 1970 was undertaken. The questions considered were the same as those used by Davis such as: 1. To analyse the dimensions of husband-wife roles into consumer purchase decisions; and 2. To determine the extent to which the husband and wife agree in their perception of roles.

The results showed the dimensions of marital roles that are essentially similar to Davis'. It also confirms Davis' contention that these roles can be differentiated further than they have been done in previous studies. The roles of each partner in the decision to purchase furniture and automobiles were measured. It was concluded that each partner recognises his role and the roles of his partner very clearly. To the marketer the data shows that sales appeals based on spouse differentiation for various product attributes are justified.

The findings of this study also indicate that the partner who is dominant for most pre-purchase decision components also tends to take the real decision to purchase. The partner who is recognised as the dominant influence actually carries this influence into the critical state to buy or not to buy [21].

Study on Family during Transitions

This study identifies the transition in household buying behaviour across a wide variety of products and services as households pass from one stage of the family life cycle to another. It analyses the role changes within the family structure during this transition and its effect on purchase decision-making. Almost all family decisions are affected by more than one of these family roles.

Transitions in the stages of the family life cycle present challenges for individuals to accept different roles within the new stage of the family life cycle. Transitions also affect the purchasing behaviour of individuals. Transitional events include birth of the first child, departure of the child from household, dissolution of marriage, death in the family, retirement, changing jobs and family relocation. These events produce a rank of anticipated stages that are equivalent to the orderly patterns of the consumers.

In this study depth interviews were conducted to collect primary data. The interview was organised as a face-to-face conversation between the interviewer and the interviewee. A convenience sample of fourteen people was selected for the depth interview. It was found through the study that the transitional flow from one stage to another proves the different buying behaviour and different family roles exist. It was found that couples1 and 2 both of whom are in the post-parenthood stage would occasionally financially support their children if requested. With couple 1, the husband is the influencer, the wife is the gatekeeper, preparer, maintainer and the disposer. Both are the deciders, buyers and users of the products. With couple 2, the husband is the influencer, preparer and maintainer while the wife is the gatekeeper and disposer. Both are buyers and users of the products.

Regarding couples 3 and 4 both of them are in the parenthood stage. The arrival of the first child makes them think for the future by saving income. Significant aspects such as insurance, baby's essentials, medical attention and income were taken into consideration to maintain their new nuclear family. The family role of consumption was generally the same between the two couples. The wife acts as the influencer, gatekeeper, maintainer and the preparer while the husband is the decider. Both are the buyer and the user.

Couple 5 is in the honeymooners stage. As young single adults, they spend their income on rent, basic home furnishings, automobiles and travel. They prepare more meals at home but continued to spend money on restaurant and entertainment and the purchase of a home. Married couples combine their income that leads to more spending power. In this case the husband is the influencer, while the wife is the disposer and they both are the gatekeepers, deciders, preparers, maintainers, buyers and users.

As regard to females 1 and 2 and males 1 and 2, these individuals moved away from their family and establishing their independence was a financial burden for them. Some bachelors spent their money on pleasure, while others intensively invested their money. The family life cycle is concerned with consumption and changes caused by the addition of family members, maturity and experience. During transitions, these events are strong enough to vary a consumer's primary life style pattern and the consumer's decision regarding products and services. The transition pattern makes the consumer prone to change and marketing intervention [22].

II

Studies on Investigation of Determinants of Joint Decision-making Under Conflicting Goals

The major studies on joint decision-making under conflicting goals are reviewed below.

Study by Davis and Rigaux

They explored the relative influence of the husband and the wife during three major phases in purchasing, namely, problem recognition, the search for information and the final decision. Interestingly there is a greater tendency for joint input during the problem recognition and final decision stages. During the problem recognition stage, the spouse may need to justify a certain purchase. Therefore they openly discuss various types of purchases which could solve the problem. This is supported by Louis Harris' study, which shows the heavy joint involvement in determining which type of goods to purchase initially. Joint involvement in the final decision stage can be caused by at least two factors. Firstly, the importance of the actual final decision has greater implications than mere information search and therefore might require greater involvement by both parties. Secondly, joint involvement helps in spreading the risk in case the decision turns out to be a poor one. Thus, one partner does not shoulder the responsibility for the decision alone.

Davis and Rigaux have classified decisions as syncratic when both the husband and wife are involved in decisions together; autonomic when decisions are usually made independently, and husband or wife-dominant when the decision to purchase was primarily influenced by one or the other [23].

Study by Corfman and Lehmann

In this study a conceptual framework is developed that provides a description of the group decision-making process in conflict situations. Selected implications of this framework as it applies to the family purchase task, are tested using experimental data provided by couples making sequences of product choice decisions. The models tested include power-related resources and power use-related goals as the determinants of relative influence. The results indicate that relative preference intensity and the outcome of preceding joint decisions consistently make the strongest contribution to relative influence [24].

Study by Menasco and Curry

In 1979 they studied the effect of different information strategies on joint decisions. The findings of the study indicate that for high-priced durable products, the husband and wife must select one multi-attribute brand from a class of such brands. The study examines the different information processing strategies on pre-choice agreement about brand utilities and post-choice utility loss for each spouse as a result of their joint decision [25].

Another study conducted by them shows how different preference structures can lead to cognitive conflict, how resolute attitudes by one spouse can modify this conflict and how persuasive messages interact with both these factors to influence a joint choice.

The findings of this study show that couples tend to choose options that are equitable and centred in their negotiation set, a tendency that is prevalent over choice occasions and bargaining conditions. The results address certain hypotheses about husband-wife choice behaviour in the context of the maximisation of dyadic utility. The results suggest that dyads tend to compromise, seeking balance and equity in outcomes. This feature was prominent in the study by conducted by Corfmann and Lehmann in 1987. Two mechanisms that support equity or balance are conflict avoidance and empathy. It was found that equity was the rule rather than the exception, that messages interact with the position of bargaining condition to influence choices for multi-attribute products or services, and that ideal positions are rarely at one extreme or the other [26].

Study by Filiatrault and Brent Ritchie

In this study, a comparison of the perceived influence within household decision-making units of different composition revealed substantial variations in the patterns of role dominance and response consensus. The result indicated that though children had relatively little perceived influence on the vacation and accommodation selection decisions, they still affected the outcome of particular choices [27].

Study by Seymour and Lessne

In this study a conflict arousal scale was developed as a tool to conduct empirical research in family decision-making. The scale's reliability and validity were examined and reported. A general overview of the scale development procedure demonstrates that the conditional influence variable is scalable. The item generation techniques allowed an adequate sampling of the conditional and the item analysis stage enabling the elimination of items that were inconsistent or non-salient. The theoretical structure of the model was recaptured in the scale development process, and the components of the conditional influence, i.e. utility, involvement, inter-personal need and power, were shown to be interpretable, salient, consistent and stable. The conflict arousal scale helps in predicting the level of conflict in an actual decision-spousal purchase situation. The major goal of this paper was to facilitate future process-oriented research on the role of conflict in family decision-making by presenting a reliable and valid scale for measuring spousal conflict arousal [28].

Spiro's Study

In this study Spiro took a sample of husband-wife pairs and asked them about a recent household durable purchase decision. 88 percent of the couples reported that they had encountered disagreement and had to undertake accommodative strategies. The husbands and wives completed separate questionnaires. Among the questions asked were items involving the "strategies" that each partner used on the other when the disagreement occurred. The results reported only low to moderate attempts to influence their partners.

Those who reported a high use of influence, seemed to try "every trick in the book" rather than rely only on one or two techniques. When the partners were asked about what their spouses had tried on them, their answers did not match with what their spouses reported that they were trying [29].

Spiro proposed and investigated six types of influence strategies to be used to persuade other family members. Depending on the product, the family members involved, and the situation, any one of these strategies may be effective. His study was based on furniture and major appliances purchases. He classified six different groups in terms of the mix of influence strategies reported. While this study did not include children's influence on the purchase, it is an interesting way to consider persuasion methods used by family members in decision-making.

Spiro investigated and proposed the following six types of influence strategies that could be used in an attempt to persuade other family members:

Expert strategy: This influence is reflected in a spouse's enumeration of specific information concerning the various alternatives. For example, one spouse can try to convince the other by arguing that he/she is more knowledgeable about the products under consideration and present detailed information about various aspects of the product to substantiate his/her claim.

Legitimate strategy: This influence deals with one spouse's attempts to influence the other's feelings of shared values concerning their role expectations. Therefore, the spouse's influence is based on the shared belief that he/she should take the decision because he/she is the husband/wife. For example the husband can argue that since he is "the man of the house," therefore he should take a particular decision. *Bargaining strategy*: This involves attempts by one spouse to turn the joint decision into an autonomous one in return for some favour granted to the other spouse. For example, in return for autonomy in a particular decision, one spouse may agree to give the other autonomy in another decision when he/she had previously refused to do so.

Reward/referent strategy: This influence is based on a combination of the reward and referent power/influence typologies. Reward influence is the influence based on an individual's ability to reward another, i.e. one spouse may be able to reward the other by doing something that the other would enjoy. Referent influence is the influence based on the identification or feeling of oneness (or desire for such an identity) of one person with another. Referent influence in marriage stems from the desire of spouses to be like their concepts of the "ideal" husband or wife.

Emotional strategy: This influence involves displaying some emotion-laden reaction. For example, some spouse may get angry with the other. These attempts are often nonverbal techniques. For example, one spouse may cry while another may use the "silent treatment".

Impression management strategy: This influence encompasses premeditated persuasive attempts to enhance one's influence differential in a dyadic relationship. For example, one spouse may claim that the other's preferred brand was "out of stock" when, in fact, it wasn't. The objective is to convince the spouse to attribute the influence attempt to external pressures beyond the influencer's control.

Nelson's Study

Nelson surveyed 284 households (only one consumer per household responded in this study) about a recent purchase conflict. She found the following four general approaches:

1. Use of negative emotion, punishments and so on, such as, refusal to do something expected of that person;
2. Use of positive emotion and subtle manipulation, such as, being especially pleasant, helpful or charming before bringing up the subject;
3. Use of withdrawal techniques, such as, refusal to discuss the issue; and
4. Use of persuasion and reason, such as, trying to convince or persuade the other person that your way is the best [30].

Park's Study

Park analysed how couples went about buying a house. He found that avoiding conflicts was an extremely important part of the overall process. In fact, instead of using, well-planned procedure (called synoptic decision-making), Park found a process that he described as muddling through.

In his study, each spouse is not quite sure of his or her own preferences in a house since it is such a complex decision. Even each spouse has little idea of what their partner prefers until they are actually going through the process. He described the resulting experience as "grouping" while striving to avoid conflict. The family believed that it made a decision jointly, when in fact it had reached a decision through disjointed, unstructured strategy [31]. The couples tried to avoid conflict on different issues. For the house characteristics, such as price, number of bedrooms, etc. the partners tried to find out which ones they agreed upon early in the process and these were set as goals. For characteristics in which one partner had expertise (kitchen, plumbing, etc.) he or she was assigned the major decision responsibility. Thirdly, when differences arose on other characteristics, the spouse who felt less strongly about the characteristic made a concession to the other about it [32].

Thus, the results of the study show that in terms of the partners decision plan themselves, both the husband and wife thought they had approached the decision in a similar way, when in fact their approaches had been quite different.

Sprey's Study

This study was conducted with the following objectives:

1. To prove that the most fruitful theoretical approach towards the study of the family and its process involves the use of a conflict framework rather than its consensus-stable equilibrium counterpart; and

2. To clarify the analytical relationships between such concepts as family stability, harmony and marital satisfaction.

The family as a system in conflict means an ongoing confrontation between its members, or between individuals with conflicting interests in their common situation. The actual occurrence of family conflict is thus incidental to this approach since it goes beyond the assertion that overt conflict or hostile interaction seems inevitable in families. Rather the position of the family members is being seen as analogous to that of players in a game. The nature of their conflict of interest thus changes with the societal definition of the game, for example, the degree to which its players can all win or lose.

Thus the family is defined as an arena in which conflicting interests and alliances of common purpose contend. The family process is thus perceived as an ongoing peace making effort, which may result in a negotiated order, a state of affairs which however remains, open to continuous re-negotiation.

Implications of the study:

1. Family harmony must be considered as a problematic rather than a normal state of affairs. The key concept in the explanation of family behaviour is thus cooperation, rather than adjustment, accommodation, or consensus. What is needed is a set of shared, mutually understood, procedural rules. The family process is not concerned with the abolition of existing differences but with their effective management.

2. Analytically speaking, conflict can be solved only through the elimination of one of the contending parties. Any given manifestation of family harmony must, therefore, be seen as a case of successful conflict management rather than as one of resolution. To explain a peaceful and orderly family process, the theoretical focus should be directed towards the explanation of the management of conflict and not, as the case often is, towards the discovery of its supposedly underlying causes.

As a last implication, it is argued that family dissolution itself, especially divorce, desertion and separation can best be explained within a framework of conflict [33].

Other Studies on Conflict in Families

Jetse Sprey has also written a paper on the management of conflict in families. The concepts developed aim to provide an analytical access to the nature of the family negotiating process. The focus is on the conceptions of bonding, aggression, appeasement and threat. In addition, the extra-marital nature of familial and marital conflict management are discussed. Throughout the argument, findings from the field of ethology are used to aid in the attempts at problem formulation [34].

Another study by Rollins and Bahr tries to clarify the various concepts in the area of marital power. The concept of power is differentiated from control attempt, control resources and authority. A theory has been developed which clarifies all these variables. It is assumed that:

1. Power and control are social interaction constructs rather than attributes of individual persons.

2. Power and control are relevant constructs only when a conflict exists between the goals of marriage partners.

3. Authority, resources and power do not exist independently of perceptions.

This theory has several unique features. It simultaneously presents theoretical constructs with reference to each participant in the social interaction, i.e. husband and wife. Secondly, it integrates constructs representing social groups and individual phenomena. Moreover, it integrates and clarifies the relationships of a series of concepts [35].

III
Studies on Changing Roles of the Wife and Children

The studies reviewed in this section primarily concentrate on the changing role of different family members and on double income families, where the wife plays an equal role in decision-making. Recently the role of children as consumers has increased at an unprecedented rate. Children do not form a homogenous group as their characteristics vary widely with respect to the age groups to which they belong. This section firstly deals with the role of children as decision-makers.

Study by Gregan and John

According to this study, children are now-a-days called upon to take decisions not only about their own purchases but also about purchases made by family unit. Not only are children spending more on snacks, sweets, toys, games and clothes, but they are also purchasing a wide range of product categories and influencing a much wider array of family purchases including items such as television, automobiles and vacations.

This study explores the emergence of adaptivity in the decision-making skills of young children. It specially focuses on young children's pre-decisional search behaviour and examines the extent to which they adapt their search behaviour to different levels of search costs and benefits in the decision environment. The results from two experiments conducted with children aged four to seven years were examined in the context of a game called a "house of prizes". The game involved making a choice between two "houses" that contained prizes hidden behind each "window". Children were allowed to search behind the windows to uncover the prizes prior to making their choices, with differing costs and benefits of doing so. The data collected on the extent of the search conducted by children of different ages suggest that the children's ability to adapt emerges during their pre-school years in a limited manner, and subsequently develops rapidly [36].

Foxman, Tansuhay and Estrom's Study

The changes in demographic and household structure have increased the impact of children on their parents' decisions and their general involvement in family decision-making. Both parents now work full-time in many households. Consequently, parents of such 'timepoor' families may permit or actively encourage their child's increased participation in family decision-making.

This study also compares the existing relationships between different family members i.e., father, mother and adolescent child, to identify the structural relationships between parents and children in family decision-making. It not only focuses on product-specific decision measures, but also includes more general measures of participation in the decision process. The product specific measures include 12 products in a broad price range, of which six are for family use and six for the adolescent's own use. The sample consisted of 161 families comprising the father, mother and adolescent child.

The results of the study indicated that children exercise some influence in the purchase decisions of a variety of products. Children have more say in the purchase of products that are less expensive and are intended for their own use. Additionally, as compared to the parents' ratings, children appeared to overstate their relative influence. One contribution to this theory comes from Blood and Wolfe (1960) and Spiro (1983), who predicted that individuals in a social unit with more resources would exercise greater influence on the decisions within that unit.

A multi-influence analysis of factors was performed to detect which patterns of divergence among family members influence perception. The analysis indicated that the mother's and father's perceptions, though not in perfect agreement, were much closer to each other than were either parent's perceptions to that of the child.

A regression analysis was also performed to investigate a variety of family structural characteristics as possible explanations for divergence in the family members' perceptions of adolescent influence. Several factors were found to significantly affect the agreement among family members regarding adolescent influence in purchase decisions. Families that exhibited greater agreement had older fathers; a concept oriented family communication style, fewer children and a mother who worked fewer hours outside the home [37].

Study by Beatty and Talpade

This study used an integrative model of teenager influence and a new scale of the perceived relative influence of younger children, when the purchases made are not for self-use. It further examined the effect of the parental employment status on teen influence as well as gender-based differences in perceptions. The teenager influence as a function of the characteristics being studied can be depicted as:

Teenager Influence = f [Teenager characteristics (Ability, Motivation) + Parental / Household Characteristics + Decision Characteristics].

In this study, the financial resources and product knowledge of the teens serve as the sources of their ability, while the perceived importance and usage of the product motivate them to influence the purchase decision. The household characteristic examined is whether the family is a dual or single income one and the decision characteristics examined include the consumption situation, the product type and decision stage.

The sample for this study consisted of 429 students of a South-eastern University, with a 90 percent response rate.

The following products were being considered for the study i.e., television, stereo, telephone and furniture. The findings show a clear connection between product importance and adolescent influence in family decision-making. The motivational or relative investment aspects, including product importance and usage, provided the most consistent explanations for the influence that teenagers believe they have in family decision-making across several products and purchase situations. However the teenagers' knowledge about the concerned product did affect their perceived influence in the search and decision process for the purchase of a stereo, which suggests that expertise does matter in the case of some products.

The teenagers' financial resources were weakly associated with influence at the initiation stage for teenager purchases but not for family purchases. The parents' dual-income status seems to allow teens greater influence for some durable purchases but not for self-purchases.

Motivational aspects, including the product importance and usage, provided the strongest and most consistent explanation of the teenagers' perceived relative influence across various stages of the purchase situation. In addition, the parental employment status positively influenced the teens' perceived influence on family durable purchases. Mothers and daughters generally did not differ in their ratings of the daughter's perceived influence on the durable purchase decision-making process, while the ratings of fathers and sons differed in terms of the son's perceived influence on the above-mentioned purchase decision [38].

Study by Green and Isabella

This study compares the family decision-making patterns under different conditions of female role perception. The findings suggest differences between contemporary and traditional families, particularly within various age and income categories. The primary objective of the study was to examine the potential impact that changes in the female role would have on the family's purchasing patterns. While the study was conducted at one point in time, making it impossible to measure the actual changes which have occurred, it is assumed that changes in the role of women are actually taking place and that these changes can be seen more in some groups of women than in others.

Role Change and Family Purchasing Patterns

A change in the sex role produces changes in family purchasing roles. The general direction of the change in purchasing roles is suggested by the notion of merging sex roles, since the husband has traditionally been the dominant economic decision-maker in the traditional families.

The sample used for the study consisted of 257 randomly selected married women who completed a self-administered questionnaire. The 10 products used in the study were groceries, furniture, major appliances, life insurance, automobile, vacation, family savings, house, selection of the family doctor and keeping track of money and bills. Separate univariate F-tests were computed between conservatives, moderates and liberals on the mean number of decisions made by the husband and wife both separately and jointly for each product and service and across all products and services. The Chi Square analysis was used to test for differences on the number of husband, wife and joint decisions made concerning the amount to be spent on each of the eight products and services.

The purchase decisions related to groceries are wife-dominated for liberals, moderates and conservatives, while decisions relating to life insurance are husband- dominated in three groups. Furniture is basically a jointly decided item, with a substantial influence exerted by the wife regardless of the prevalent attitudes towards the women's role. The decisions pertaining to family savings are split between joint and husband decisions across the groups. Finally, housing decisions tend to be jointly made in all the three groups [39].

Study by Scott Ward and Daniel Wackman

The present study examines the impact of three variables on children's purchase influence attempts and parental yielding, viz. demographics, parent-child interaction and mothers' mass communication behaviour. In this study self-administered questionnaires were sent to 132 mothers of children in the age group of 5-12 years. The sample was skewed towards the upper and upper-middle classes.

Two kinds of analysis were used. Firstly, age group differences were compared by means and percentages for three age groups. Here no overall statistical test was used because no single test was appropriate. Moreover, zero-order and partial correlations were computed to examine the relationships between various independent variables and dependent variables.

Mothers were asked to indicate the frequency of their child's purchase influence attempts for 22 products categorised as relevant foods, less relevant foods, durable products for child use, lotions and toiletries and other products. All products varied in terms of price, the frequency of purchase, and relevance to the child with relation to consumption or use by other family members. An analysis of the marginal data indicated that the influence of children tends to decrease with age, depending on the type of product, but that of mothers yielding to requests increases with age, probably reflecting a perceived increase in the competence of older children to make judgements about purchase decisions.

It was found that the influence of children in purchases varies across product categories. It was the most frequent for food products and followed by durable products for child use. Since the incidence of mothers yielding was found to be higher for food products, it indicated that children who ask for food products get them more often than those demanding other products.

The various aspects of parent-child conflict are thus related to influence attempts and yielding. The data suggests that influence attempts may be part of a more general parent-child conflict; and that mothers who restrict viewing are unlikely to yield to the purchase influence attempts. Finally, the time spent by mothers watching television is positively related only to influence attempts. Mothers with positive attitudes towards advertising are more likely to yield to influence attempts than mothers with negative attitudes. No relationship was, however, observed between purchase influence attempts and parental yielding (dependent variables), on one hand, and the number of children in the family and social class, on the other [40].

Study by Carron and Scott Ward

Andre Caron and Scott Ward examined certain aspects of the relative influence of mass media and interpersonal sources on children's purchase desires and parental decision-making pertaining to their children's product desires.

It was found that all the children requested for mostly the same kind of products irrespective of their age or social class. The product category requested most often was non-interactive toys (accounting for 23 percent of all requests), followed by sports goods (18 percent), competition toys (14 percent) and clothing (13 percent) respectively.

Television was the most frequent source of information, followed by friends. While these patterns showed minor variations in terms of social class or sex, the source of information for the product idea changed with the age of the child. In general, older children cited television as their source of information more often than younger children did.

Requests for gifts declined with the age of the child. However, the conversion rate of these children (into those receiving specifically requested gifts) was not as high as that for older children. Middle class children made more requests and consequently received more gifts than did upper class children. The type of gift requested varied significantly for social class groups and also with the age of the child but not significantly by the sex of the child.

In terms of the responses of parents to their children's requests for gifts, there were few differences over social class and age groups. Most often the parents responded in neutral terms regardless of the specific item asked for. The responses found among the middle class respondents were slightly more negative than those among their upper class counterparts.

Both middle and upper class children received mostly what they requested. Younger children received mostly non-interactive toys and competition games, while the older children largely got clothing. Girls received different items than did the boys. Parental yielding to requests varied over social class and also by the type of item requested [41].

Study by Szybillo and Tenenbein

This study tries to explore how the family role structure inclusive of children, varies over sub-decisions taken within a generic service category, for instance, a choice made between a fast food restaurant and a conventional restaurant. An analysis of family role structures during the entire process of decision-making for the choice of the restaurant showed a high degree of adult-child interaction for all stages of decision-making, i.e., initiation of purchase, supply of information on alternatives, and the final decision.

Within each decision stage, the data indicated more husband-wife involvement for the conventional restaurant decision than for the fast food restaurant decision. In the case of the fast food restaurant, the adult child interaction was again high (72 percent of all role structures) for sub-decisions like when and what type of restaurant to go to for dinner, except for the sub-decision regarding 'money to spend', wherein the adult only category pre-dominated.

An analysis of the family role structure across the decisions over the choice of restaurant within each sub-decision also indicated that children's involvement was greater in the case of the fast food restaurant than for the conventional restaurant. There was greater joint decision-making by the husband and wife for the conventional restaurant rather than for the fast food restaurant. This finding was also evident in case of the sub-decision regarding the type of restaurant chosen, but the overall level of the joint husband and wife decision-making process decreased as the children became involved [42].

Study by Burr and Burr

This study was conducted to find out how parents respond when asked by children to buy products as a result of communication directed at the children. It was found that the disposition of the parents to buy as a result of various appeals used by the children varies according to the appeal used.

Parents are more likely to buy the desired product if the child wants the prize premium attached to it or when the child says that he saw it on television. Appeals like "others use it" are the least influential. Even "health appeals" were found to have less influence as effective communication tools used by the child when requesting for parental purchases.

Parents usually combine the "saw it on television" appeal with more information like economy of purchase, ease of use of the product, etc., whereas in the case of premiums they think that the request is not unreasonable and someone would eventually consume the product in the family [43].

Nickelodeon's Separate Research Studies

Three separate research studies on American children, commissioned by Nickelodeon, have all come to the same conclusion that today kids are exerting unprecedented influence over the purchasing decisions made in their families, including decisions for non kid specific products such as computer hardware and software. The survey also indicates that kids as young as six years of age are exhibiting a distinct awareness of brands.

The studies conducted separately for Nickelodeon by Penn, Schoen and Berland Associates, Inc., IntelliQuest and The NPD Group, Inc. all found that the current generation of kids aged 6-14 years are exerting a greater influence on their parents' purchase behaviour than ever before [44]. Overall, the research concluded that children significantly influence parental purchase decisions in a large range of categories. According to the Penn, Schoen and Berland study, an average of 43 percent of the total purchases within the wide range of categories studied are influenced by children. The major findings of the these studies are:

1. As regards the computer and technology areas, 40 percent of the current computer owners said that their child had some influence on the purchase decision of the home PC. Nearly nine in ten parents said that their child's brand preference in the technology category carries some importance for them, while 30 percent said that it carried major importance. The data also indicates parents' growing awareness and acceptance of the fact that even young children have significant knowledge about brands and are reliable sources for the latter. The study found that computer buyers allow their children to exercise a great deal of influence over the purchase decision. An incredible 71 percent of the parents who plan to purchase computers this year said that their children would influence their purchase.

2. All the three surveys suggested that children as young as six years of age are distinctly aware of brands, particularly in the clothing and computer categories. 39 percent of the parents said that they believe their children know more than themselves about categories such as sports, drinks and juices.

3. Within the apparel industry, 80 percent of the parents said that their 6-11 year-olds influence clothing purchases, and 76 percent said that their 6-11 year olds influence footwear purchases.

4. More than 85 percent of the kids and parents surveyed said that they go to shopping malls together. And while they are there, 67 percent of the kids get items that they ask for. Additionally, 80 percent of the kids get the items that they ask for at the supermarket, with 8 out of 10 kids getting items they ask for from various stores. 92 percent of the parents said that they let kids pick things for themselves

while shopping including clothes, cold drinks, CDs/tapes, footwear, school supplies, books and magazines.

5. It was found through the study that brand awareness increases with age in most categories, especially in the case of those products that children start buying for themselves, like computer games, clothing and hygiene products such as toothpaste and shampoo.

The Penn, Schoen and Berland study was based on a total of 1200 interviews with parents and children conducted at shopping malls throughout the country during the period, October 5-16, 1998. The IntelliQuest study was based on telephone interviews during November-December, 1998 with 400 households currently owning or planning to buy a personal computer within the next year. The NPD Group study included 1204 telephone interviews conducted with parents of children aged 6-14 years and focused on the influence exercised by kids on apparel purchases in their family.

Study by Reynold and Wells

A study conducted by Wells in 1965 found that children play an influencing role in family purchases. This takes place in various ways, viz. 1) by making personal purchases; 2) by making direct requests in the store; 3) by making direct requests at home; and 4) by passive dictation.

Wells found that when children get small amounts of pocket money or some money from gifts, they spend it on personal purchases, i.e. on products like candy, gum, inexpensive toys, etc., which are considered as 'extras' by parents. As younger children were often taken along for shopping, they made more requests than older ones in the store. But all their requests were not acceded to. Older children were more selective while making requests, had greater influence in the purchase decision and were treated as full members of the family.

At home, younger children (in the 5-7 age group) asked more for things that they saw on television, especially toys and cereals. Older children made fewer requests but they were still influential. Even if they did not ask for specific brands, parents knew what they liked and disliked and made the purchases accordingly [45].

Study by Wells and Loscuito

In this study, Wells and Loscuito used spot observations to study the purchase behaviour of shoppers in various supermarkets of Northern Jersey. They found that children accompany their parents while shopping and also exert influence on the purchases when they were present at the shops. The products chosen for the study were cereal, candy and detergent.

It was found that the degree of children's influence varied according to the product category. The children's influence was found to be the strongest at the cereal counter, was distinct at the candy counter and was present to some degree at the detergent display. Although only three-fifths of the children attempted to influence cereal selection, in more than half the cases, the child was successful in obtaining the desired cereal.

Suburban parents were found to be more indulgent of their children than urban parents except for the purchase of candy. The study revealed that a suburban child makes more attempts to influence his parents' purchase decision and except in the case of candy, he succeeds in higher proportion than his urban counterparts [46].

Study by Berey and Pollay

In this study, Berey and Pollay investigated the child's influence on consumer decisions by studying the interaction between mother and child for the product class of 'ready to eat breakfast cereals'. The extent of the child's influence on his parents' decision was taken to be dependent on at least two factors: the child's assertiveness and the parent's child centredness.

It was found that the mother's purchase behaviour was independent of: 1) the child's age; 2) the number of children in the home; 3) her own (the mother's) employment outside the home; 4) the number of trips that the child made alone to the store; and 5) the number of trips that the child made to the store accompanied by his mother.

The mother's child-centredness was found to be negatively related to her purchase of the child's favourite cereal. Highly child-centred mothers purchased their children's preferred cereals less frequently. They were more concerned about what is right and healthy for their children. On the other hand, mothers showing less child-centredness displayed a greater tendency to purchase their children's preferred cereals.

The child's degree of assertiveness was found to have little effect on his mother's decision to purchase the child's favourite cereal. But a significant relationship was found to exist between the child's assertiveness and mother's child-centredness. The mother's brand recall of her child's favourite cereal was also significantly related to her purchase of these cereals. A more positive relationship between the mother's brand recall and the child's assertiveness leads to some increase in brand recall. The mother's child-centredness was negatively related to her brand recall of her child's favourite cereal, which indicates that the mother acts as a strong gatekeeper during the selection of products by her child [47].

IV

Studies on Family Decision-making in India

In India, a number of studies have been undertaken to identify the impact of various demographic factors like income, occupation, age, etc. on consumer behaviour, but very few research studies have assessed the role played by various family members in the purchase of a product.

Study on Role of Family in Consumer Purchase Decisions

A study undertaken by N. K. Aggarwalla examines the dimensions of husband-wife interaction in the purchase of durable and semi-durable products. Four products have been chosen for the study viz. television, furniture, crockery and woollen garments. The questionnaire method was used as a tool for conducting the survey and data was collected from 100 families in each product category. The following influence patterns were used as bases for collecting the data [48]:

1. Only the husband decided.
2. Only the wife decided.
3. Both the husband and wife decided.
4. The husband influenced the decision.
5. The wife influenced the decision.
6. Any other person influenced the decision.

The findings in case of durables including television and furniture, support the hypothesis that the influence exerted by husbands is considerably higher than that of their wives. In approximately 50 percent of the cases, it was observed that the husband exercised more influence than his wife.

This was followed by a joint decision taken together by both the husband and wife. The children's influence was found to be negligible in the purchase of television and furniture.

In case of crockery, the wife's dominance in taking decisions was observed in a majority of the cases. The influence of the husband alone or jointly with the wife was found to be equal in only about one-fifth of the cases selected for the study. These findings were consistent with the hypothesis that the influence exerted by wives was fairly higher than that of their husbands in the purchase of crockery.

The findings of the study reject the hypothesis that in case of the purchase of woollen garments, the husband and wife together act as a group have more influence than as an individual. The analysis showed that in about 35 percent of the cases, the wife as an individual dominated all decisions except those relating to store/dealer selection and the amount to be spent.

As in the case of durables, the influence of children on the purchase decisions of semi- durable products was found to be insignificant. Persons under the 'others' category also did not exercise much influence except in the case of the purchase of television.

Thus, in this study an attempt has been made to determine the extent of the agreement between the husband and the wife in purchase decisions. Further, the study illustrates how the perceptions of the wife and husband, as individuals and as groups, are influenced by variations in age, income, qualification and occupation of the respondents.

Study on Indian Youth

For this study, 100 young consumers from Delhi University were selected for analysis. The questionnaire method was used to collect data and some of the findings of the survey are as follows [49]:

1. *Pocket allowance vis-a-vis expenditure pattern*: The young consumers experience an elevation in their spending capacity on joining college. Since they have immense spending capacities, they provide the marketers with an absorbing market. The amount available to these young consumers in the form of pocket allowance is positively correlated (+0.465) to their family incomes. The money received by these young consumers is spent on definite items, viz. eatables, conveyance and travelling, cosmetics, jewellery, cigarettes, magazines, etc.

2. *Marketing variables and the young consumers*: The 4 P's of marketing affect the youth in the following ways:

(a) Price: Young consumers with significant spending power claim that the price of a product plays a major role in the purchase decision. However, they do not give undue importance to price-related factors such as low price, discounts, etc. in the purchase decision but insist on the importance of quality and style in a product. Thus, it can be inferred that young consumers look for quality and style at reasonable prices.

(b) Product: Young consumers exhibit brand loyalty for certain items including cigarettes, beverages, footwear and cosmetics, among other similar product categories. New products also attract the attention of these young consumers, who wish to use and adopt these products as soon as they are seen in the market or are seen being used by someone. Young consumers, in general, do not give much importance to attractive packaging of the product, if its quality is not satisfactory.

(a) Promotion: Young consumers believe that advertisements, in general, do not provide information on the price of the product. These consumers like advertisements because they provide information on the availability of the product and are enjoyable.

(b) Place or Physical Distribution: Significant point-of-sale features that attract the young buyers and make shopping enjoyable for them are the provision of quality products, vast variety of products, polite and helpful salespeople, and fair and competitive prices. Greater consumer satisfaction can thus be ensured by making the goods available to the consumer through retail outlets offering quality products, a variety of goods, polite and helpful sales personnel and competitive prices.

3. *Young consumers as influenced by various persons and as influencers of family purchase decisions:* A large majority of young consumers perceive themselves to be pragmatically independent while taking a purchase decision. But 60 percent of them abided by the suggestions made by others. In the purchase decision of young consumers, parents and friends exercise greater influence on them in comparison to shopkeepers and advertisement models.

A large majority of the young consumers often influence the purchase decisions of their family. Among the items for which they give their suggestions are entertainment and music system, decorative items, furniture, household goods and electrical appliances.

4. *Reading and television interests of the young consumers*: All the respondents read newspapers/magazines though there were some variations in what each individual read. The contents of the print media that attract the youth,

in general, are news items, theatre and movie reviews, horoscope, sports, fashion columns, comics, puzzles and games. Marketers who wish to target the youth market should therefore place their advertisements on pages with these contents.

Study on Purchasing Patterns of Urban Consumer

The present study was confined to the analysis of purchasing patterns of adolescent consumers, by certain chosen variables as type of product, income class, age and sex. The study analysed the extent of the freedom enjoyed by adolescent consumers in their purchasing role structures.

The scope of the study was restricted to the urban educated adolescents in the age group of 13-20 years, residing in the Union Territory of Delhi. The study was undertaken for ten product categories, which were classified as convenience goods, shopping goods and speciality goods. A study of the expenditure patterns of adolescent consumers revealed some interesting trends of which one pertains to the per capita expenditure of adolescents. It was found that the per capita expenditure incurred on higher-class adolescent consumers was the highest, followed by the middle and lower class adolescent consumers.

The expenditure patterns of adolescent consumers highlighted a suggestive trend. While the convenience and shopping goods were used/consumed by all adolescent consumers, this was not the case with speciality goods. were not used/consumed by all adolescent consumers.

An analysis of the purchasing role structures of adolescent consumers by type of product found significant variations across the selected products. While the adolescent consumers exhibited a mixed pattern of purchasing freedom in the convenience and speciality goods categories, there was a significant dependence on the family for shopping goods.

A positive relationship between the income class and the purchasing role structure of adolescents was found to exist only for two of the product groups in the speciality goods category viz. cassettes and novels/comics). Irrespective of the income class, the study also found that the dominance of family is significantly higher in cases wherein the product either entails a high socio-economic risk or affects the physical welfare of adolescent consumers.

Variations in purchasing patterns of adolescents were also studied in relation to variables such as age, sex, clothing, behaviour of adolescents and per capita expenditure on clothing.

On the basis of the trends/patterns found by the present study, the following suggestions have been proposed to the marketers, in particular to the retailer. Since the adolescent market is a potential one-both at present and in the future, retailers should plan their marketing strategy not only to tap the growing market but also to suitably modify their present product lines with a change in the interests, fashions and lifestyles of the adolescent consumers [50].

Study on Dimensions of Marital Roles

This study is based on nuclear families residing in Delhi, which are engaged in a business or profession. An arbitrary number of 50 families was chosen as the sample size with a total number of 100 questionnaires distributed to collect data for analysis. Since in one family two questionnaires were being filled, the distinction between the two questionnaires was maintained by giving a white questionnaire to the husband and a yellow one to the wife. it was made yellow.

The respondents were interviewed individually except in one case where four families were interviewed together. Before the questionnaire was handed out, there was a brief discussion during which the purpose of the study was revealed to the respondents and their free and frank opinions obtained.

A non-disguised structured questionnaire was used for the study. The various attributes for which the data was classified included age, education and income. The various components of the questionnaire were:

1. Who went for purchasing?
2. Who initiated the idea of purchase?
3. Who allocated the amount to be spent on the purchase of such items?
4. Who selected the shop?
5. Who decided the brand?

For each of the above components of the decision, the following three dimensions of influences were considered: a) Husband-dominated; b) Wife-dominated; and c) Syncratic.

An analysis of the data showed that in a majority of the families, it was the wife who perceived the need and initiated the process for the purchase of a semi-durable product, followed by the joint involvement of the spouses and at the end, by the husband alone. Most of the allocation task was handled by the husbands alone, followed by a situation wherein the husbands consulted their wives and the last where wives could come for this job. As regards the selection of the store, the families wherein the wife alone could take this decision were maximum in number, while the number of joint decision-making families was less. On the whole thus wife domination constituted the largest influence followed by joint involvement and husband domination came in only at the end.

In the case of durable products the overall purchase was still followed by purchases made jointly by both the spouses. As far as the initiation of the idea for purchase of these durable products was concerned, husband dominance was found to be prominent followed by wife dominance and joint dominance, which were almost equal. The traditional role of the husband as an allocator of funds was retained as it was found that sometimes he takes this decision in consultation with his wife. The husband also dominated the decision pertaining to the selection of the store. The ultimate decision to purchase was taken by the husband alone in a majority of the cases [51].

Study on Children's Buying Behaviour

The present study confines itself to the analysis of children's influence in consumer buying behaviour and how factors like income of the family, age of the child, sex of the child, mother's educational qualifications and her employment status affect such influence. It also analyses the purchasing independence enjoyed by children.

The study shows that children, in general, make less frequent purchase requests. Children's purchase requests decline, as the product becomes less relevant to them. Mothers in general "frequently" yield to the children's purchase requests. The mothers' yielding declines, as the product becomes more expensive. Children in the age group of 5-7 years and 8-10 years, in general make more purchase requests than children in the age group of 11-12 years.

Boys make more purchase requests than girls for products which provide entertainment irrespective of the fact whether the product is more relevant to the children or is a family product. Girls make more brand-specific requests than boys for eatables and drinks. The education of the mother also affects the children's brand- specific requests. Children of employed mothers make comparatively more brand-specific requests than those of unemployed mothers.

An important factor which emerges from the study is that while promoting their products, marketers should focus on both the mothers and their children. They also need to vary their strategies depending on age, the extent to which the mother yields and the product, as the case may be.

The development of suitable marketing strategies also necessitates, among other things, segmenting the market by relating, say the category of more brand- specific purchase requests to the demographic data of families to which such children belong [52].

Study by Ammirati Puris Lintas (APL) P:SNAP on Woman

Pathfinders, the market research wing of the leading advertising agency, Lintas, carried out an extensive study on the urban woman consumer. The first study of this series was released in 1987. This is the third study of the Nation's Attitudes and Psychographics (P:SNAP) released in October, 1997 [53]. The objective of the study was to develop a database of lifestyles and psychographical information across women from chosen target segments. The research agency and advertisers felt the need to look beyond the mere demographics of age, income and sex, commonly used as benchmarks prior to this study.

In this study, the target segment comprised urban Indian housewives in towns with populations of 5,000 and above. The study aimed at identifying a means of segmenting that would give a better understanding of the targeted segment.

The objective of the study was to define clusters of urban women according to their beliefs, attitudes and lifestyles in addition to their demographic profiles. The objective was accomplished by identifying groups of consumers who are likely to behave similarly towards products or services and who follow similar lifestyles.

A study of this kind helps the advertiser to plan more effective strategies to reach target markets if he knows more about its consumers in terms of how the consumers live, their interests and what they like. The woman was specifically chosen for the study because more often, in an urban situation, it is the woman who makes the buying decision. The study also helps in identifying the aspirations and fantasies of the target audience and whether users of a particular brand are attitudinally different from the non-users.

Moreover, the study has tracked eight clusters of woman and has also made a comparison with the results obtained in 1987 with those obtained in 1993. Women have been variously classified as troubled homebody, tightfisted traditionalist, contended conservative, gregarious hedonist, archetypal provider, anxious rebel, contemporary housewife and affluent sophisticated professional.

The first category of woman called **troubled homebody** is characterised as one with a large family size, young motherhood, high proportion of widows, low Monthly Household Income (MHI) and educational levels, low media penetration and high pessimism. The 1987 study showed that 15.9 percent of the respondents fell into this category which increased to18.3 percent in 1993.

The second category of woman called **tightfisted traditionalist** comprises housewives who are above 40 years of age, with low to middle Monthly Household

Income (MHI), high family consciousness, insular and introvert lifestyle, thrift and economy-focused character. The 1987 study showed that 14.8 percent of the respondents fell into that category which dropped to 10 percent in 1993.

The third category of woman is named as **contended conservative** who is defined as having larger than average families with older children, characterised by insular lifestyles except in the case of food habits, early marriage and middle income level. The 1987 study showed that there were 7 percent respondents in this category, which increased to 9.3 percent in 1993.

The fourth category of woman is named as **gregarious hedonist** who is more likely to be working. She has liberal food habits, believes she is successful and her personal life is more important than family. She's an extrovert who indulges herself and uses all personal products. The 1987 study showed that there were 8.7 percent respondents in this category, which came down to 6.6 percent in 1993.

The fifth category of woman is named as **archetypal provider** who is more gregarious and prone to top outside influence. Women in this category take pride in looking after the house with low servant usage. They are characterised by a high level of affluence and of penetration of consumer durables. The 1987 study showed that there were 13 percent respondents in this category, which came down to 8.8 percent in 1993.

The sixth category of woman is named as **anxious rebel** which includes women who are better educated, with the desire to study and work but who are pessimists and not satisfied with their lot. There is a high penetration of mixers, grinders and two-in-ones among women in this category. The 1987 study showed that there were 14.1

percent respondents in this category which increased to 15.8 percent in 1993.

The seventh category of woman is named as **contemporary housewife** who is well-educated, working and hence accounts for a double income. She has a more active lifestyle, has high level of investments and makes use of servants. She's highly optimistic and is into all types of media. The 1987 study showed that there were 19.2 percent respondents in this category which increased to 22.1 percent in 1993.

The eighth category of woman is named as **affluent sophisticated professional** who is the most self-assured and confident of all clusters. She's defined as one who has married late, usually works full-time and her education and investment levels are high. She even reads English newspapers and magazines. The 1987 study showed that there were 7.3 percent respondents in this category, which increased to 9.1 percent in 1993.

Shifts between these clusters give an indication of societal movements. This study has come out with certain trends regarding Indian families by taking one member of the family i.e. the woman into perspective. The study also puts into perspective the differences between a SEC A1 class and a SEC A2 class. It also highlights the subtle differences in lifestyle between these categories.

Study on the Urban Indian Woman

A survey by Pulse, the consumer insight cell of McCann Erickson, brings out some interesting insights on the changes which are increasingly being seen in the Indian woman. The survey is part of an ongoing research programme [54].

The Indian woman, as she is represented in various media, including advertising, films and television, seems to be emerging as a more decisive person, who is breaking out of the shadows of traditional dependence and playing a more proactive role in her own family.

Pulse, the proprietary consumer insights cell of the advertising agency, McCann Erickson, that does cultural mapping on an ongoing basis in India and abroad, conducted focus group interviews among urban Indian middle class women with the objective of relating the findings to brand communications to facilitate greater efficacy of the latter.

The first phase of cultural mapping of the urban Indian woman was conducted between August 1997 and January 1998 through a number of focus groups across Delhi, Mumbai, Calcutta and Chennai. The focus groups covered women from SECs, A&B and women professionals from SEC A1 in the age group 25-35 years. A few 50-plus mothers-in-law were also asked certain questions in this regard. An important result which has emerged from the first phase of the study is that the Indian woman has traditionally lived with a state of mind that can be evocatively be termed as "acceptance anxiety". This arose from the cultural archetypes that were virtually created and built for her by her country's cultural ethos such as arranged marriage, continued alienation, valuing expectations and caring nature. These cultural archetypes are reflected in her social archetypes wherein she is expected to play the pre-determined roles of a mother, a daughter-in-law, a wife or that of a daughter, a sister or a virgin, over which she has little control. The traditional roles that an Indian woman is thus expected to play during her lifespan are those of the dutiful daughter, the homely daughter-in-law, and the adjusting wife, the sacrificing mother, the dominating mother-in-law, and the unworldly widow.

The most overwhelming change, however, which has taken place recently for the Indian woman has been in the sphere of education. Even in the B1& B2 groups, the level and penetration of education revealed by the study has been very astonishing. It was found through the study that the Indian woman is hesitant to play the various roles expected of her. This hesitation is due to the lack of a corresponding change in the social infrastructure around the Indian woman, resulting in a new set of factors including her more conscious and as yet unrealised yearnings and desires for love, happiness and enjoyment.

Consequently, the Indian woman's state of mind has moved from 'acceptance anxiety' to 'acceptance angst' reflected in oft-quoted statements such as: "You are always doing so many things for so many people. I would like somebody to look after me the way I would like to be looked after." These statements add strength to the hypothesis that the cultural and social archetypal roles of the Indian woman have not changed much over a period of time and that .the expectations from her still remain the same. She still continues to play and accept her traditionally determined roles in life. This has given rise to a new age woman who is really dual-faced. She exercises greater control over her own life, reflected in a changed power equation within the family and a legitimate authority over her own domain.

The new Indian woman has a strong desire for personal achievement, reflected in her need to work outside the home and in her anxiety not to be called "the typical housewife" and to make her children embodiments of her personal achievement. The significant factor is the woman's changing relationship with her children reflected in the following trends: a) The children continue to occupy centre-stage in the woman's life; b) But the children are no longer her lifeline to legitimacy as they were in her traditional life role; c) There is an isolation of responsibility from the family's children to "my children" as families are becoming more nuclear and as the woman now plays a more active role in her children's development.

However, while the woman is more in control of the relationship she wants to build with her children, she still yearns for more intimate interaction with her husband. He continues to remain a shadowy presence in her life, while she feels an increasing need to share, to belong. This is because the husband's expectations from his wife have not changed and his role in her life still remains ambiguous. The duality of her conventional roles and her simultaneous growing self-awareness has thus brought the Indian woman face-to-face with a new set of dilemmas. There is a constant questioning of her own 'usefulness'.

Significantly, the study reveals that among the working women in the SEC A1 category, those earning less than their husbands and those working out of economic need, showed the same response as that of other women. There was no recognition of their economic contribution because of their jobs. The common claim was that they were going out to work because they wanted to, and not to earn money. This attitude possibly arises out of a sense of guilt of resulting from their imagined 'self indulgence' and more often than not, because there is no active appreciation of the woman's achievements beyond her traditional life roles.

So while there is a profound change in the way a woman sees herself today in terms of an enhancement of her self-esteem and self-confidence, at the same time, there is also a lack of adequate social mechanisms required to handle this change. Realistically then, while the new age Indian woman experiences a growing optimism resulting from her enhanced self-respect, she also yearns for the fulfillment of her personal desires. Symbolically, while the dividing line of her expected roles still remains deeply etched around her, there is more latitude in the new definition of her roles.

Thus the fundamental change in today's Indian woman is that there is a sense of personal identity. Communication strategies should therefore take these trends into consideration. In the case of the new age Indian woman, both her emerging confidence as well as her angst on the lack of support to her emerging sense of self should be addressed.

Study on Buying Motives and Role Played by Various Family Members

According to Nabankur Gupta, Sales and Marketing Director, Videocon International, every time a purchase is made, there are two kinds of motives behind it: the rational and the emotional. No purchase decision is totally rational or totally emotional. A shift is taking place today in the balance of emotions in purchase decisions. Ten years ago, if a family needed a refrigerator at home, it was the man of the house that did the research and the SWOT analysis, before settling for a purchase. His decision was rational and final. Almost as many years ago, the decision to buy a shampoo brand was definitely an emotional one. According to Mr. Gupta, there is a change in the buying patterns of families as for low-ticket items, the purchase decisions are getting increasingly rational, and with high-ticket items, they are getting increasingly emotional. But again the buying formula is not as simple and is influenced by a lot of factors.

It is a fact that for a lot of high-ticket items, such as TVs, refrigerators, and washing machines, the purchase decisions are being made by the families today. If one individual in the family carries more influence than the others, then he/she decides, emotionally, which brand he/she wants. People also try to force a rational reconfirmation from friends and neighbours even though these people may have no exposure to that brand.

Amongst the low-ticket items, such as FMCGs, mostly individual decisions are taken. With no one to lean on for a decision, the individual tends to be rational in his choice. If a high-ticket item requires an individual decision, the buyer would look for strong rational reasons to support an initial emotional choice. If in a family, there are two strong decision influencers, a compromise is likely to take place on the brand choice [55].

Study by McCann Pulse

McCann Pulse has undertaken a study on the consumer's reactions, expectations and ambitions in markets across Asia. The study analysed the buying behaviour of the middle class. Some of the major findings of the study were:

1. In a middle class the **youth** population takes for granted a certain security of expectation. They 'know' that they would get a good education and the job they want and that it would not be a 'job for life' but a stepping stone to an entrepreneurial future. They know that reaching the right school is more important than learning itself. They know, understand and endeavour to fulfil their parent's expectations.

2. The **teenage** period has also become longer as the children of the new middle class stay in school longer, putting off the process of decision-making as much as

possible. They willingly share their parents' vision and put in extra efforts to become self-reliant.

3. The role of **mothers** is also being redefined in a multitude of ways. Mothers always focus on their family's success through their children to the point of self-sacrifice; they are now reconsidering what it takes to be a good mother. Across the entire Asian region, mothers now say that they not only want a comfortable and respected relationship with their husband but also a romantic one.

4. **Fathers** are being seen not just as respected family heads but also as increasingly distant figures drawn to work for longer hours away from the family apartment. The fastest growing and most potent consumer group in Asia is the new ageing middle class. This constitutes the 45-year plus generation that pioneered the advent of the mass middle class. This generation has seen the gradual move to abandon the extended family home, who are able to focus the benefits of a successful life on fewer children and grand-children while expecting to live longer themselves. This has forced the consumer to reconsider choices and has fostered a renewed commitment to the family unit [56].

Study on Children

In a study, Outlook Research Pacific surveyed 769 families with household incomes of over Rs. 10,000 per month and at least one child between the age group of 5 and 14 years [57. Some of the questions that the respondents were asked and the corresponding responses were:

Q. 1. How do kids react to advertisements aimed at them?

82.1 percent kids start wanting the products seeing the particular advertisements.

Q. 2. Do such advertisements sell products not meant for children?

67.1 percent agreed with the statement, while 19 percent disagreed with it, 10.7 percent expressed no opinion about it and 3.3 percent said that they didn't know about it.

Q. 3. Do children waste money on unnecessary products?

73.9 percent were found to waste money.

Q. 4. Are Advertisements and gifts making children eat too much junk food?

74.3 percent agreed with this statement, while 25.7 percent disagreed with it.

Q. 5. Should there be laws for advertisements addressed to kids?

57 percent agreed on the need for such laws, while 25.6 percent didn't agree.

Q. 6. Is American culture-influencing children?

65.6 percent agreed with this statement, while 15 percent didn't.

Q. 7. Are children turning more consumerist?

72.5 percent agreed with this contention, while 14.9 percent did not.

This study was conducted to understand how kids influence the purchase of certain items such as chocolates, snacks and other low value items in which they are interested.

Studies on Indian Youth

Various advertising agencies have conducted separate studies on the buying behaviour of Indian youth. Youth marketing conventionally means creating a peer group for the youth to identify with. Some of the research studies on Indian youth are:

Study by ORG-MARG: There are supposed to be 150 million 12-to-19 year-olds in India. But if seen demographically, the picture is very disappointing. The population of rich youth (social class A1) in the top 23 towns is 0.5 million. If we add the creamy layer A to this, we get a total of 1.4 million, and if to this figure, we also add the consuming classes A and B, the total is 4 million. The study revealed that the total number of youth in urban India in classes A and B is 10.6 million, which is still far short of 150 million. If to this are added the urban poor, viz. classes C, D and E, the resultant total is 32.2 million. Research has shown that the urban-rich youth market is under-exploited, limited not so much by money as by imagination which can help decide what products and services can actually offer great value, giving the youth reason to buy them. The 12-to-19 year old youth is a major consumer of everyday mainstream consumer products. The IRS study reveals that 28 to 32 percent of the products here are actually consumed by them. The study conducted by ORG-MARG also concluded that the youth market is very important. Today's youth are clearly tomorrow's mainstream consumers. Marketers should invest in them since today's poor youth would actually be able to consume tomorrow. In emerging societies people don't have to wait to have incomes before deciding on their brand preferences; they decide their brand choices today and when they get rich they stick with these choices. It was found that the youth market is partly adult, partly baby, partly time-warped, and partly futuristic. From the above listed reasons, it is obvious why youth marketing should be regarded as a mainstream activity rather than merely as a niche for speciality products [58].

Comments from the Youth Marketing Forum by Ms. Vidyarthi, Manager, Quest: According to Ms. Vidyarthi, the youth is clearly a creation of the marketplace, a result of liberalisation and the opening up of the skies to satellite television and Internet. The marketers should not forget the existence of Indian culture and should see how Indian youth with their traditional background read and interpret the communication addressed to them.

Indian youth is being driven by three factors. These are firstly, a need to be accepted by peers, secondly, a need to have their parents' approval of their choices and thirdly, a need to be taken seriously by adults. Today's Indian youth have started choosing between the 'traditional and Western' and try to be just themselves.

Most Indian youth confess to wearing two faces, i.e. a public face and a family face. Interestingly, while the public face is supposed to be 'put on' to conform to social pressures, the family face is just the opposite. Most of the youth feel they are themselves in the company of their peers, and it is at home that they behave as they are expected to. Thus, Indian youth should be taken seriously and the future communications should be designed after considering the above-mentioned factors [59].

Summary

The focus of the above studies has been on family consumption decision. While numerous studies focus on the role played by the husband or wife in a purchase situation the role of children on household decision-making has largely been ignored. No specific study has been conducted to find out how Indian families purchase a consumer durable product so as to warrant different marketing and communication strategies. In order to bridge this gap in this important area of marketing the present study was undertaken.

Notes

1. Elizabeth M. Wolgast , "Do Husbands or Wives Make the Purchasing Decisions?", ***Journal of Marketing***, Vol. 23 (October 1958), pp. 152-158.

2. ***ibid***, pp. 156-158.

3. Cynthia Webster, "Effects of Hispanic Ethnic Identification on Marital Roles in the Purchase Decision Process", ***Journal of Consumer Research***, Vol. 21 (September 1994), pp. 319-331.

4. William J. Qualls, "Household Decision Behaviour : The Impact of Husbands and Wives Sex Role Orientation", ***Journal of Consumer Research***, Vol. 14 (September 1987), pp. 264-279.

5. Mirra Komarovsky, "Class Differences in Family Decision-Making", ***Consumer Behaviour: Household Decision-Making***, (Nelson N. Foot, University Press, NewYork, 1961), pp. 225-265.

6. Harry L. Davis, Stephen J. Hoch and E. K. Easton Ragsdale, "An Anchoring and Adjustment Model of Spousal Predictions", ***Journal of Consumer Research***, Vol. 13 (June 1986), pp. 25-37.

7. H. Sharp and P. Mott, "Consumer Decisions in the Metropolitan Family", ***Journal of Marketing***, Vol. 21 (October 1956), pp. 149-156.

8. Robert Ferber and Lucy Chao Lee, "Husband-Wife Influence in Family Purchasing Behaviour", ***Journal of Consumer Research***, (June 1974), pp. 43-50.

9. Robert Ferber, "Family Decision-Making and Economic Behaviour", in E.B. Scheldon (Philadelphia: J.B. Lippincott Company, 1973), in ***Family Economic Behaviour, Problems_and Prospects***, pp. 39-41.

10. Robert Ferber, "On the Reliability of Responses Secured in Sample Surveys", ***Journal of the American_Statistical Association***, Vol. 50 (September 1955), pp. 788-810.

11. Donald J. Hempel, " Family Buying Decisions : A Cross-Cultural Perspective", ***Journal of Marketing Research***, Vol. 11 (August 1974), pp. 295-302.

12. Robert O. Blood and Donald M. Wolfe, ***Husbands and Wives: The Dynamics of Married Living*** (The Free Press, Ill., USA, 1960), pp. 12-28.

13. Isabella C. M. Cunningham and Robert T Green, "Purchasing Roles in the U.S. Family: 1955 and 1973", ***Journal of Marketing***, *Vol.* 38 (October 1974), pp. 61-64.

14. Bernert Eleanor Sheldon, "Family Decision-Making and Economic Behaviour", ***Family Economic Behaviour: Problems and Prospects*** (J. B. Lippincott Co., Toronto 1972), pp. 39-41.

15. H. Sharp and P. Mott, "Consumer Decisions in the Metropolitan Family", ***Journal of Marketing***, Vol. 21 (October 1956), pp. 149-156.

16. Robert Ferber, "Research on Household Behaviour", ***American Economic Review***, Vol. 52 (March 1962), pp. 19-63.

17. Zober Martin, ***Marketing Management*** (John Wiley and Sons, New York, 1964), pp. 353-356.

18. Paul D Converse and Harvey W Huegy, ***The Elements of Marketing***, 3rd ed. (Prentice-Hall, Englewood Cliffs, N.J., 1972), pp. 31-32.

19. Robert E. Wilkie, "Husband-Wife Influence in Purchase Decisions - A Confirmation and Extension", ***Journal of Marketing Research***, Vol. 12 (May 1975), pp. 224-227.

20. Harry L. Davis, "Dimensions of Marital Roles in Consumer Decision Making", ***Journal of Marketing Research***, Vol. 7 (May 1970), pp.168-177.

21. F.K. Shuptrine and G. Samuelson, "Dimensions of Marital Roles in Consumer Decision- Making: Revisited", ***Journal of Marketing Research***, Vol. 13 (February 1976), pp. 87-91.

22. "Family During Transitions", obtained from **http.lycos.com**.

23. Harry L. Davis and Benny P. Rigaux, "Perception of Marital Roles in Decision Processes", ***Journal of Consumer Research***, Vol. 1 (June 1974), pp. 51-62.

24. Kim P. Corfman.and Donald R. Lehmann, "Models of Cooperative Group Decision-Making and Relative Influence: An Experimental Investigation of Family Purchase Decisions", ***Journal of Consumer Research***, Vol. 14 (June 1987), pp. 1-13.

25. David J. Curry and Michael B. Menasco, "Some Effects of Differing Information Processing Strategies on Husband-Wife Joint Decisions, ***Journal of Consumer Research***, Vol. 6 (September 1979), pp. 192-203.

26. Michael B. Menasco and David J. Curry, "Utility and Choice: An Empirical study of Wife/Husband Decision-Making", ***Journal of Consumer Research***, Vol. 16 (June 1989),
pp. 87-96.

27. Pierre Filiatrault and J. R. Brent Ritchie, "Joint Purchasing Decisions: A Comparison of Influence Structure in Family and Couple Decision-Making Units", ***Journal of Consumer Research,*** Vol. 7 (September 1980), pp. 131-140.

28. Daniel Seymour and Greg Lessne, "Spousal Conflict Arousal: Scale Development", ***Journal of Consumer Research***, Vol. 11 (December 1984), pp. 810-821.

29. Rosann L. Spiro, "Persuasion in Family Decision-Making", ***Journal of Consumer Research***, (March 1983), pp. 393-402.

30. Margaret C. Nelson, "The Resolution of Conflict in Joint Purchase Decisions by Husbands And Wives: A Review and Empirical Test", ***Advances in Consumer Research***, Vol. 15 (1988), pp. 436-441 in William L. Wilkie, "Household Influences", ***Consumer Behaviour,*** 3rd ed. (Wiley International Edition, New York, 1994), p. 404.

31. Whan C. Park, "Joint Decisions in Home Purchasing: A Muddling-Through Process", ***Journal of Consumer Research***, Vol. 9 (September 1982), pp. 151-162.

32. Whan C. Park, "A Conflict Resolution Choice Model", ***Journal of Consumer Research***, Vol. 5 (September 1978), pp. 124-135.

33. Jetse Sprey, "The Family as a System in Conflict", ***Journal of Marriage and the Family*** (November 1969), pp. 699- 706.

34. Jetse Sprey, "On the Management of Conflict in Families", ***Journal of Marriage and the Family***, 1971, pp. 722-731.

35. Rollins C. Boyd and Stephen J. Bahr, "A Theory of Power Relationships in Marriage", ***Journal of Marriage and the Family***, November 1976, pp. 619-627.

36. Jennifer Gregan Paxton, and John Deborah Roedder, "Are Young Children Adaptive Decision Makers: A Study of Age Differences in Information Search Behaviour", ***Journal of Consumer Research***, Vol.21 (March 1995), pp. 567-579.

37. Ellen R. Foxman, Patriya S. Tansuhaj and Karin M. Ekstrom, "Family Member's Perceptions of Adolescents Influence in Family Decision-Making", ***Journal of Consumer Research***, Vol. 14 (March 1989), pp. 482- 491.

38. Sharon E. Beatty and Salil Talpade, "Adolescent Influence in Family Decision-Making: A Replication with Extension", ***Journal of Consumer Research***, Vol. 21 (September 1994), pp. 332-341.

39. Robert T.Green, and Isabella C. M. Cunningham, " Feminine Role Perception and Family Purchasing Decisions", ***Journal of Marketing Research***, Vol. 12 (August 1975), pp. 325-332.

40. Scott Ward and Daniel Wackman, "Children Purchase Influence Attempts and Parental Yielding", ***Journal of Marketing Research***, Vol. 9 (August 1972), pp. 316-319.

41. Andre Carron and Scott Ward, "Gift Decisions by Kids and Parents", ***Journal of Advertising Research***, Vol. 15 (August 1975), pp. 15-20.

42. George J Szybillo, Sosanie, Arlene K and Tenenbein, Aron, "Should Children Be Seen but Not Heard", ***Journal of Advertising Research***, Vol. 17 (December 1977), pp. 7-13.

43. Burr, Pat L and Burr, Richard M, "Parental Responses to Child Marketing", ***Journal of Advertising Research,*** Vol. 17 (December 1977), pp. 17-20.

44. Nickelodeon, "Separate Research Studies Indicate Today's Kids Having Unprecedented Influence On Family Purchasing Decisions", ***http://www.businesswire.com/webbox/bw.020899/1098564.htm***, December, 1999, pp. 1-3.

45. Fred D. Reynolds and William D. Wells, ***Consumer Behaviour*** (McGraw-Hill Book Company, 1977), pp. 49-74.

46. William D. Wells and Loscuito, Leonard , "Direct Observation of Purchasing Behaviour", ***Journal of Marketing Research***, Vol. 3 (August 1966), pp. 227-233.

47. Lewis A. Berey, and Richard W Pollay, " The Influencing Role of Child in Family Decision-Making", ***Journal of Marketing Research***, Vol. 5 (February 1968), pp. 70-72.

48. N. K. Aggarwala, ***Role of Family in Consumer Purchase Decisions***, Unpublished M. Phil. Dissertation, Delhi University, Department of Commerce, April 1978.

49. Madhu Kashyap, ***Buying Behaviour of College Students: An Analysis of Youth Market***, Unpublished M. Phil. Dissertation, Delhi University, Department of Commerce, 1985.

50. Mani Arul Nandhi, ***Purchasing Patterns of Adolescent Consumers***, Unpublished M. Phil. Dissertation, Delhi University, Department of Commerce, 1983.

51. Keshav Gupta, ***Dimensions of Marital Roles in Purchase Decisions***, Unpublished M. Phil. Dissertation, April, Delhi University, Department of Commerce, 1979.

52. Poonam, ***Children Influence in Consumer Buying Behaviour***, Unpublished M. Phil. Dissertation, Delhi University, Department of Commerce, August 1991.

53. Bharati Rawla, "What Makes Her Tick", ***The Economic Times: 'Brand Equity'***, October 8-14, 1997, p. 3.

54. Lopa Banerjee, "Living Life on Hold", ***The Economic Times: 'Brand Equity'***, February 27, 1998, p. 3.

55. Nabankur Gupta, "The Buying Emotion", ***The Economic Times: 'Brand Equity'***, December 16, 1998, p. 1.

56. McCann, Pulse, "Future Tense", ***The Economic Times: 'Brand Equity'***, January 11, 2000, p. 3.

57. Neerja Jetley, "Child is the Father of Marketing", ***Outlook***, March 1, 1999, pp. 78-82.

58. Rama Bijapurkar, "Youth Un-niched", ***The Economic Times: 'Brand Equity'***, April 6, 1999, p. 3.

59. Indrani Vidyarthi, "But Seriously, We are the Youth", ***The Economic Times: 'Brand Equity'***, April 6, 1999, p. 2.

3

Family Decision-making Process: An Overview

This chapter introduces the methodology used for conducting the study. It also describes the scope, research design and methodology used for collecting information, as also the techniques employed for data analysis.

The present study analyses, the family decision-making process and the roles played by family members in the purchase of different durable products. A majority of consumer studies classify family consumption decisions as husband-dominated, wife-dominated, joint or autonomous. The extent and nature of the husband or wife's influence in family decisions depends on the specific product or service, the particular stage in the decision-making process and the specific features under consideration.

In India, despite much cultural diversity, the structure of families shows uniformity, to a large extent. At the same time, the cultural and other values inculcated in children in India during their upbringing make the Indian families vastly different from their counterparts in the West. This study attempts to capture the dynamics of the family decision-making process in case of specific product categories. In our society, family-related roles are constantly changing. For instance, today a substantial number of married women are working outside the house. In view of all these factors, it was decided to study the family roles in depth.

Furthermore, most research studies on family decision-making have focussed only on direct influence and have ignored the indirect influence of various other members present in the family. In a family decision, different members are likely to focus on the specific attributes that are, most relevant to them. A child may evaluate the colour and style of a bicycle while one or both parents may evaluate its price, warranty and safety features. Therefore, in this study, questions are asked from all the members of the family who have been actively involved in playing a particular role. Ferber has noted that each family member's reply should be treated as an individual opinion rather than a collective one [1].

It was further found that most of the existing research primarily focuses on the role played by the husband or the wife in a purchase situation, where the purchase is considered as an act rather than a process. In the past, the focus used to be on the decision-maker's role; what goes on before that, such as the role of the initiator or influencer and the actions of the buyer and user after they have taken a decision to purchase the product have not been studied in the past.

Most of the earlier studies have thus focussed not on household decision-making but on husband-wife decision-making. The role of children in decision-making has largely been ignored, even though children exert a substantial influence in the consumption process [2]. The following two factors were thus considered while the study was being conducted:

1. For analysing different roles, viz., those of the initiator, influencer, decider, buyer and user, the family members who had actually played that particular role were interviewed.

2. Only the families who had actually purchased the respective product were selected for the study and no hypothetical purchase situation was considered. Earlier studies had revealed that in case of a hypothetical situation,

as for example, different members of a family were to be asked what roles they would play if the family had to buy a car, it was found that families were not able to answer such questions properly.

Why Study Family Influence?

Even when members of a family are leading their own lives and, pursuing their own dreams, and when their tastes are different, the bond that exists between them continues to be very strong. This is mainly because of the following three reasons:

1. The consumption of a product may be personal, but its choice is not. Every family member looks for the approval and ratification of his choice from the other members. For example, a father may not buy a pair of sneakers if his son does not approve of it. Or a wife would not buy a dress if her husband does not approve of it.

2. Often the family consumption decisions are dependent on one another. In most families, the needs of various members as also their desire to purchase new products cannot be satisfied by the family's limited income. This necessitates an allocation of family resources and a trade-off among all the desired products and services.

3. Many products are purchased for the collective use and consumption of the family. This is because the traditional boundaries between the roles assigned to the different members of the family often disappear.

Significance of Understanding the Family Decision-Making Process

Various studies have proved that family has a strong influence on consumption behaviour. Therefore the real target customer for the marketer is not the man or the woman, nor the child in isolation, but the family as a whole. And the critical component of the marketing mix used to effectively target members of the family is product promotion. It is for this reason that brands focusing on the family are doing well in the Indian market. For instance the advertisement for Nestle's Maggi soup always shows the whole family sitting around the table united in its fondness for the product; while to sell its paints, Asian Paints uses a commercial where the husband and his mother welcome the new-born and his young mother. And to sell its detergents, Surf Excel shows the mother endorsing the detergent with references to her children, her husband and the family dynamics; Hyundai is promoting Santro as the complete family car. The three major reasons, which necessitate an understanding of the family decision-making process, are given below.

Changing Characteristics of Indian Families

The break-up of the joint and extended family has played a significant role in the emergence of the new urban family as a customer. According to a survey conducted by ***Business Today*** in 1971, the average urban family in India consisted of 5.46 members, where individuals had little room for bonding. In contrast in 1997, this average came down to only 4.6 members. This reduction in the size of the family has enabled the members of a family to relate better to one another and still enjoy their own space [3]. The major reasons responsible for these changes are given below:

(a) Shift from strictly hierarchical to egalitarian character of the family: Indian families are experiencing many changes and are moving from being strictly hierarchical to egalitarian in character. Earlier, the age and gender of the family members governed the authority.

Purchase decisions, including the brand chosen, rested with the eldest male member, especially since he alone had the financial power. Other members of the family rarely had a say in such purchase decisions and could express their desire only through the proper channel.

In today's scenario, however, all the members, by and large, have the right to express their views and eventually influence the purchase decision through their choices. As a result, financial independence rests with all family members, at least to some extent. The general awareness level of all the members is also reasonably high.

(b) The media explosion: With the Indian skies opening up to various television channels, consumers are being increasingly exposed to a wide range of product information.

a. Increasing peer influence: More and more families are now becoming double-income families with the wife going out to work. While this enhances the purchasing power of women, it also exposes them to phenomenal peer pressure, which, in turn, influences their purchase decision.

Relevance to the Marketer

In several marketing situations, it is the family and not the individual that should be considered as a unit of consumption while developing the marketing plan, particularly when the goods are of common usage, such as breakfast cereal and a television set, or when the purchase decision involves a high financial commitment, as in the case of a car or in cases where the product/brand used by one member affects the entire family, such as a local or branded airconditioner used in the home.

The knowledge of family influences is often very important for developing appropriate marketing strategies.

There are at least three major reasons for analysing families from the perspective of marketing strategy [4].

A. Once it is recognised that the same individual may not perform all the purchase or consumption tasks, it becomes clear that the development of a successful marketing mix depends on answers to the following questions:

(a) Is the product likely to be purchased for individual or joint family use? For example, an electric shaver is purchased for an individual's use but a TV set is meant for all the members of the family.

(b) Is the product likely to be purchased with an individual's or with the family's funds? With the number of earning members in the family increasing, the money for major purchases usually comes from a joint pool.

(c) Is the product so expensive that its purchase involves an important trade-off in purchasing other products for the family? For example, the wife's decision to purchase a new washing machine may delay the purchase of an audio system for the family.

(d) Are family members likely to disagree about the perceived value of the product? The son's demand for a three CD changer audio system may be shot down and a single CD double cassette recorder may be preferred by other family members.

(e) Is the product likely to be used by more than one family member? If so, are product modifications necessary to accommodate the different person's viewpoints? For example, a TV set should have a front socket for video games if there are children at home.

(f) Which family members will influence the purchase and what media and messages should be used to appeal to each of them?

(g) Is a particular store preferred by family members or by various families in the target market?

B. The second reason why the family analysis is important for marketing strategy development is the long-term influence of the family purchasing patterns on children's behaviour. Parents teach children, both directly and through observation, why, how, when, where and what to purchase.

C. The third reason for the importance of family analysis for developing an appropriate marketing strategy is the immense influence that children exert on the budget allocation and the purchase or consumption behaviour of the family. For instance, with the arrival of a child in the family, several products that were never considered earlier are purchased [5].

Sociologists have long been concerned with the study of families, and their work has been the foundation for research on the consumer behaviour of families.

Product Selection

Based on the focus group discussions and review of the past literature, consumer durable products can be classified into the following categories, depending upon which family member uses a particular product the most:

(i) Equal usage: If the product is used equally by most members of the family, for example television and furniture.

(ii) Wife - primary user: If it is used primarily by the wife, for example washing machine and refrigerator.

(iii) Husband - primary user: If it is used primarily by the husband, for example car.

(iv) Children - primary users: If it is used primarily by the children, for example audio system and personal computer.

Six consumer durable products have been chosen for the study. These are audio system, car, personal computer, refrigerator, television and washing machine. The roles of the different family members in the purchase decision are likely to change in keeping with the nature of the product being purchased.

The following criteria were considered for selecting the above products:

1. The purchase of these products represents an important decision in the concerned families, as all the members are involved in the purchase decision in some way or the other.

2. All these products have been considered for research work in the past.

3. The purchase of these products involves a substantial financial outlay.

4. The purchase of these products also carries social importance.

The families, who had purchased at least one of the selected durable products within three months before the questionnaire was administered, were used for the purpose of the study.

The family as a sampling unit was considered for the purpose of the study. Profile of the respondents is summarised in Table 3.1.

313 families who had recently purchased one of the six durable products were successfully contacted. The members of these families were further identified as initiators, influencers, deciders, buyers and users of the product(s). Additional data was also collected separately to pinpoint the family characteristics of each respondent who had actively played a particular role in the buying decision. If two members from a family had actively played a particular role, then both the members were considered as respondents for

the purpose of the study. In the following chapters, each buying role including the characteristics of respondents who have played that role have been considered separately.

Table 3.1: Profile of Respondents

Member	Role				
	Initiator	Influencer	Decider	Buyer	User
Husband	69 (19.7)	140 (29.9)	230 (71.7)	247 (76.5)	163 (21.2)
Wife	131 (37.3)	137 (29.3)	41 (12.8)	22 (6.8)	216 (28.1)
Child-1	107 (30.5)	120 (25.6)	31 (9.7)	33 (10.2)	179 (23.3)
Child-2	32 (9.1)	38 (8.1)	5 (1.6)	6 (1.9)	108 (14.1)
Child-3	2 (.6)	2 (.4)	-	-	29 (3.8)
Grand Father	1 (.3)	11 (2.4)	12 (3.7)	8 (2.5)	20 (2.6)
Grand Mother	4 (1.1)	7 (1.5)	-	1 (.3)	21 (2.7)
Member A	5 (1.4)	11 (2.4)	2 (.6)	6 (1.9)	25 (3.3)
Member B	-	2 (.4)	-	-	7 (.9)
Total	351 (100.0)	468 (100.0)	321 (100.0)	323 (100.0)	768 (100.0)

Note: Figures in parentheses represent the percentages

Table 3.1 shows the sample profile of respondents. Husbands played the more active role of deciders and buyers for the purchase of a durable product. As regards initiators, children played the most active role, followed by the wives. The maximum respondents were user (768), followed by influencers (468), initiators (351), buyers (323) and deciders (321).

Family Size

The 313 families considered for the analysis were of varying sizes. These family sizes are shown in Table 3.2.

Table 3.2: Distribution of Respondents by Family Size

Family Size	Frequency	Percent
Two	42	13.4
Three	71	22.6
Four	107	34.2
Five	59	18.8
> Six	34	10.9
Total	313	100.0

As shown in the table, the majority of families that were surveyed for the purpose of study consisted of four members each, followed by families of three members. After that a family size of five members was found. This pattern is similar to those of a survey conducted by ORG called the Indian Readership Survey, 1995 covering both urban and rural India, which revealed that 74 percent of the Indian households are nuclear and that a typical family across urban and rural India consists of 3.9 individuals [6].

Monthly Household Income

All the 313 families who had recently purchased one of the durable products belong to various income categories. The monthly household income of the families is shown in Table 3.3.

Table 3.3: Distribution of Respondents by Monthly Household Income

Monthly Household Income (Rs.)	Frequency	Percent
Up to 10,000	37	11.8
10,001 – 15,000	56	17.8
15,001 – 20,000	83	26.6
20,001 – 25,000	53	17.0
More than 25,000	84	26.8
Total	313	100.0

The table reveals that majority of the families who had recently purchased a durable product either fall in more than 25,000 (26.8 percent) or in the 15,000-20,000 (26.6 percent)-income bracket. This is being followed by families having a monthly household income of 10,001-15,000 (17.8 percent) and 20,001-25,000 (17.0 percent). There are only 11.8 percent families which have a monthly household income up to 10,000.

Summary

An attempt has been made to complement various past studies regarding family buying behaviour. Main objective of this study is to analyse the various buying roles. All the members of selected families who had played a particular role in the buying process were interviewed. Each role has been analysed for different products with respect to demographic characteristics of the members. The statistical tools used for the purpose of the study have also been spelt in this chapter.

Notes

1. Robert Ferber, "On The Reliability of Responses Secured in Sample Surveys", ***Journal of the American Statistical Association***, September 1955, pp.788-810.

2. Del I. Hawkins, *et al*, ***Consumer Behaviour: Implications for Marketing Strategy***, 3rd ed. (Business Publications, USA, 1986), pp. 276-284.

3. Shailesh Dobhal, "Selling to the New Urban Family", ***Business Today***, February 22, 1999, pp. 66-81.

4. Peter J. Paul and Olson C. Jerry, ***Consumer Behaviour: Marketing Strategy Perspectives*** (Richard D. Irwin, Homewood, Ill., 1987), pp. 447-451.

5. Malika Rodrigues, "Kids Play", ***The Economic Times: 'Brand Equity'***, August 23-29, 2000, p.3.

6. Polomy Dhawan, "Clues to Change: IRS 1995", ***Advertising and Marketing***, Vol. 15, March 1996, pp. 24-31.

4

Buying Roles: The Initiator

In the context of the buying decision, the initiator is a person who is the first to suggest the idea of buying a particular product or service. Any member of the family can express the need for a product or service. Quite often, the product in question will not merely be for the initiator's personal use only but will be used by the entire family. The husband may not be satisfied with the quality of the clothes washed by the maid. He can therefore initiate the process for the purchase of a washing machine. The need for a particular product in a family may remain latent till it is triggered by certain internal or external stimuli. Internally, some of the normal needs may rise to a threshold level and become a 'drive' when one or more of the members express the desire to buy the product and the thought is shared among different family members. Externally, various stimuli such as advertisements or word of mouth publicity can lead to the initiation process by one or more members in the family. Initiator as a role is played right in the beginning of the decision-making process at the 'Need Recognition' stage.

Need Recognition →	Information Search →	Evaluation of Alternatives →	Purchase Decision →	Post-purchase Behaviour
Initiators				

The nature of the consumer durable product to be purchased and the demographic characteristics (sex, age, level of education, income etc.) of the concerned family members govern the behaviour of the initiators. It is hence important to identify the initiators for different products.

Since we are referring to a conglomeration of related people in a family, their interactions are worth studying. The initiators are likely to express their need first to a) the person who is most likely to fulfil the need, or b) the member who is most easily accessible as defined by the family structure or traditions. The role that this member plays in the subsequent decision-making process explains the choice of the initiating members.

The actual time taken to finally purchase the product ever since the initiators actually started the process is worth finding. Also important is whether the proposal for the same product was turned down in the past and some other product was given a higher priority.

The reasons mentioned for suggesting the purchase of the product point to the level of the needs to be fulfilled. Finally, the satisfaction achieved by the initiators from the purchased product shows how the influence of other members in the decision-making process can be used for interpreting the basic requirement.

As mentioned in the beginning, all the above aspects need to be studied in relation to the demographic characteristics of the initiator members and the type of the product under consideration, in order to obtain a clear picture.

The different roles played by various family members are discussed in depth in the current and following chapters. Family decision-making is a complex process and Indian families exhibit quite different characteristics as compared to their counterparts in Western societies thereby rendering Western studies on this topic somewhat irrelevant in the Indian context. In India, family bonds are very strong and since each purchase of a consumer durable product entails a substantial expense, many family members are inevitably involved in the decision-making process.

Characteristics of the Initiator

It was found that 351 family members have acted as initiators. In some of the families, more than one member acted as initiators. Hence, the number of initiators turns out to be more than the total number of families surveyed. The characteristics of initiator-members are shown in Table 4.1.

Table 4.1:Characteristics of Initiators (Respondents)

Characteristics	Frequency	Percent
SEX		
Male	146	41.6
Female	205	58.4
AGE		
Less than 18 years	46	13.1
19-25 years	102	29.1
26-35 years	92	26.2
36-50 years	77	21.9
More than 50 years	34	9.7
EDUCATION		
< XII	59	16.8
Graduate	132	37.6
Post Graduate	100	28.5
Professional e.g., MBBS,	60	17.1
OCCUPATION		
Government Service	51	14.5
Own Business	32	9.1
Self Employed Professional	26	7.4
Working in Private Concern	53	15.1
Retired	8	2.3
Housewife	81	23.1
Student	100	28.5

As shown in the table that a typical initiator in a family, planning to purchase a consumer durable product is most likely to be young (19-35 years), well-educated (graduate or post-graduate), female member who is either a student or a housewife by profession. The major inferences that can be drawn from the table regarding the role of an initiator are as follows.

Women in the house take on the responsibility of being the homemaker. Traditionally also women decide about the items to be added in the household, decoration and the upkeep of the house. Although we have not dealt with the issue of the decorative value of the consumer durable products in the study, it is a known fact that in Indian homes consumer durable products are as much a showpiece as they are functional objects. Refrigerators particularly are rarely placed in the kitchen and are usually given a prime place in the drawing room. It applies for the televisions and the audio systems as well. It is no surprise then that around 60 percent of the women take on the role of the initiator. Around 40 percent of these women initiators are the housewives, which corroborates the fact that women indeed are the homemakers in Indian homes.

Persons who have taken up the role of initiator are quite well educated (83.2 percent are either graduates or post-graduates or professionals). 55.3 percent of all initiators are in the age group of 19-35 years. Both these factors (age and education) signify that these are mature persons in the family.

Member-wise Status of Initiators

The member-wise status of the initiators is shown in Table 4.2. The table reveals the distribution with respect to the status of the initiator member in the family. Children in that context refer to the next generation family members and there is no reflection on their age. The table shows that the role of the initiator is clearly dominated by wife and children. Husbands are initiators in only 19.4 percent of

Table 4.2: Member-wise Status of Initiators

Member	Frequency	Percent
Husband	68	19.4
Wife	131	37.3
Child 1	108	30.8
Child 2	32	9.1
Child 3	2	0.6
Grand father	1	0.3
Grand mother	4	1.1
Member A	5	1.4
Total	351	100.0

the cases. Grandparents as initiators are a mere 1.4 percent allowing us to deduce that it is the younger members in the family who shall initiate the process of purchase. Involvement of different member in the role of an initiator reflects on the openness that exists in the Indian family where any member of the family may express their need with regard to a consumer durable product.

Initiator Member vis-à-vis the Product Purchased

A cross tabulation between the initiator member vis-à-vis the product purchased was done in order to know which family members initiate the purchase process for different products. This is shown in Table 4.3. Children have clearly emerged as single largest initiator member for the audio system (68.3 percent), personal computers (68.6 percent) and television (57.6 percent). They are also important co-initiators for the purchase of a car (37.2 percent).

Table 4.3: Initiator Member vis-à-vis Product Purchased

Product Purchased	**No. of Initiator Members**			
	Husband	Wife	Children and others #	Total
Audio system	10 (16.7)	9 (15.0)	41 (68.3)	60 (100.0)
Car	25 (42.3)	12 (20.3)	22 (37.2)	59 (100.0)
Personal Computer	13 (25.4)	5 (9.8)	33 (64.7)	51 (100.0)
Refrigerator	5 (8.3)	47 (81.7)	8 (13.3)	60 (100.0)
Television	9 (15.2)	16 (27.1)	34 (57.6)	59 (100.0)
Washing Machine	8 (12.9)	42 (67.8)	12 (19.35)	62 (100.0)
Total	70 (19.9)	131 (37.3)	152 (42.7)	351 (100.0)
Chi-square =140.46**				

**Significant at 0.01 level.
Figures in parentheses represent the percents
#'Others' represent grandparents etc. whose frequency is taken along with 'children'.

Wife has been the single largest initiator for refrigerators (81.7 percent) and washing machines (67.8 percent) whereas the husband has been a prominent initiating member only in the case of cars (42.3 percent). Apart from these products husband and wife have been relatively dormant in their role as initiator.

The same is true for children for certain product categories. This is responsible for chi-square value showing a significant difference in the product purchased and the initiating member.

Above findings can help categorise the consumer durable products depending upon which members are the main beneficiaries. It can be assumed that the persons who are going to be benefited the most are likely to express their desire first among different members in the family. Based on this the marketers of different consumer durable products can plan their communication strategy. At the same time product design and services can be modified in different products.

Mentioning the Product's Need to a Particular Family Member

Once a family member feels the need for a product it is likely that other members are also going to be affected by the purchase. The initiating member is expected to share his/her views with other members as well. The desire is likely to be disclosed to the members who are either expected to support the decision or who are going to be instrumental in purchasing the product. This aspect discloses an important aspect of the dynamics of the family decision-making. It also shows which family member is considered to be most easily approachable. Family members with whom the initiators shared their need for the consumer durable product are shown in Table 4.4.

Table 4.4: Mentioning the Product's Need to a Particular Family Member
(N = 351)

Member	Frequency	Percent
Husband	219	62.4
Wife	122	34.8
Child 1	41	11.7
Child 2	24	6.8
Child 3	5	1.4
Grand father	19	5.4
Grand mother	8	2.3
Member A	9	2.6

Note: Multiple Answers

The table reveals that the initiating members are most likely to first share their need for a consumer durable product with the husband followed by the wife. It can be deduced from Table 4.4 in conjunction with table 4.2 that most husbands and wives have shared their need with each other but more children have preferred father over their mother for expressing their requirement. It may then be deduced that in the Indian families husband is still the breadwinner and moreover he is more approachable unlike the traditional paternal figure.

Time Taken in Actual Purchase of the Product

All the 351 initiating members were asked the time span between their mentioning about the need of the product and the actual purchase. The total time taken in purchasing the above mentioned six durable products i.e., audio system, car, personal computer, refrigerator, television, washing machine is shown in Table 4.5.

Table 4.5: Time Taken in Actual Purchase of Product

Actual Time Taken	Frequency	Percent
Less than Two Weeks	98	27.9
Two weeks - One Month	76	21.7
One - Two Months	65	18.5
More than Two Months	112	31.9
Total	351	100.0

It can be deduced from the table that the average time taken to make the purchase since the need was first mentioned, is around six weeks. Time taken by a family in purchase of a consumer durable product is an important factor in the decision-making process and hence warrants more detailed study as to how this factor is related to other variables such as the demographic profile of initiators and type of product under consideration.

Time Taken vis-à-vis Income

Income and the average price of the product purchased are other factors that influence the time taken in the decision-making process in the purchase of a consumer durable product. A cross tabulation of time taken *vis-à-vis* income of initiators is shown in Table 4.6.

Table 4.6 depicts that the average time taken to purchase the product is relatively lower in case of families with monthly household income less than Rs. 10,000 (1.26 months) and with monthly household income more than Rs. 25,000 (1.19 months). For families having monthly household income between Rs. 10,001-25,000 average time taken in all three groups is around 1.49 months. chi-square value, which is significant at 0.05 level shows that monthly household income and the time taken to purchase the product differ significantly. This observation can be interpreted as follows.

Table 4.6: Time Taken in Purchase Decision vis-à-vis Income

Monthly Household Income (Rs.)	Average Price of Product (Rs.)	Average Time Taken for Purchase (Months	Actual Time Taken				
			< 2 W	2 W-1 M	1 - 2 M	> 2 M	Total
< = 10,000	18,848	1.26	15 (35.7)	8 (19.0)	8 (19.0)	11 (26.2)	42 (100.0)
10,001-15,000	38,377	1.49	13 (21.7)	13 (21.7)	12 (20.0)	22 (36.7)	60 (100.0)
15,001-20,000	63,386	1.45	29 (31.5)	15 (16.3)	12 (13.0)	36 (39.1)	92 (100.0)
20,001-25,000	86,835	1.52	11 (18.6)	10 (16.9)	18 (30.5)	20 (33.9)	59 (100.0)
> 25,000	87,506	1.19	30 (30.6)	30 (30.6)	15 (15.3)	23 (23.5)	98 (100.0)
Total			98 (27.9)	76 (21.7)	65 (18.5)	112 (31.9)	351 (100.0)
Chi-square = 21.15*							

*Significant at 0.05 level; W=week, M=month.
Note: Figures in parentheses represent the percentages

Families with income less than Rs. 10,000 take lesser time because the average price of the product purchased is also relatively lower at Rs. 18,848. Second group that takes relatively lower time has monthly income of more than Rs. 25,000. It is probably because the perceived risk (ratio of the price of product purchased and average income) is lower for this high income segment with more disposable income that they take lower time to purchase.

Groups which take more time to purchase actually belong to the middle income level (Rs. 10,001-25,000) and the price of the product purchased is also on the higher side, ranging between Rs. 38,000-86,000. The perceived risk (ratio of the price of product purchased and average income) is hence relatively higher for these groups.

Time Taken vis-à-vis Age of Initiators

Age is another factor, which influences the time taken in decision-making. A cross tabulation between time taken vis-à-vis age of initiators is shown in Table 4.7.

Table 4.7: Time Taken in Purchase Decision vis-à-vis Age of Initiators

Age	Average Time Taken to Purchase (months)	Actual Time Taken				
		< =2 Weeks	2 Weeks – 1 Month	1 - 2 Months	> 2 Months	Total
< =18 years	1.60	7 (15.2)	10 (21.7)	10 (21.7)	19 (41.3)	46 (100.0)
19-25 years	1.33	31 (30.4)	21 (20.6)	21 (20.6)	29 (28.4)	102 (100.0)
26-35 years	1.27	25 (27.2)	24 (26.1)	21 (22.8)	22 (23.9)	92 (100.0)
36-50 years	1.56	19 (24.7)	14 (18.2)	10 (13.0)	34 (44.2)	77 (100.0)
> 50 years	1.11	16 (47.1)	7 (20.6)	3 (8.8)	8 (23.5)	34 (100.0)
Total		98 (27.9)	76 (21.7)	65 (18.5)	112 (31.9)	351(100.0)
chi-square = 21.27*						

*Significant at 0.05 level.
Note: Figures in parentheses represent the percentages

It can be seen from Table 4.7 that the time taken to purchase the consumer durable product in case of the young initiators (age <=18 years) is the highest at 1.6 months. These members, below the age of 18 years are not likely to be the earning members in a family. Requirement for a high value product from them is likely to be considered after a lot of discussion and will require a large amount of convincing from them.

Time taken to purchase a consumer durable product is also relatively higher (1.56 months) in case of initiating members in the age group of 36-50 years. A relatively senior member at this stage is more likely to suggest for a replacement of an old product. More time is expected to be taken when a case of replacement of possibly a fully functional product is under consideration.

For initiators in the age groups 19-25 years and 26-35, years time taken is at a relatively lower level at 1.33 and 1.27 months respectively. These initiators are the earning members in the family are in the process of adding new products in the household. Need for the products is clear and after some evaluation and trade-offs the products are likely to be purchased.

Least amount of time is taken in the case of initiators who are senior citizens (age > 50 years). At the peek of their careers, or recently retired, these members are financially sound and likely to contribute funds for the purchase. At the same time, the products suggested are likely to be first or second replacements when the present products have more or less become non-operational and the decision to replace is easy. Finally, suggestions from the senior members are given due respect in the Indian families. The time taken to make the purchase of the products need for which is expressed by the initiators in this age group is hence lesser. chi-square value, which is significant at 0.05 level shows that age and the time taken to purchase the product differ significantly.

Time Taken vis-à-vis Education of initiators

As with other demographic variables, we shall see if there is a relationship between the education of initiating members and the time taken in the decision-making process for the purchase of a consumer durable product. The time taken vis-à-vis education of initiators is shown in Table 4.8.

Table 4.8: Time Taken vis-à-vis Education of Initiators

Education	Actual Time Taken				
	< =2 Weeks	2 Weeks – 1 Month	1 - 2 Months	> 2 Months	Total
< XII	14 (23.7)	9 (15.3)	11 (18.6)	25 (42.4)	59 (100.0)
Graduate	40 (30.3)	29 (22.0)	27 (20.5)	36 (27.3)	132 (100.0)
Post Graduate	26 (26.0)	24 (24.0)	17 (17.0)	33 (33.0)	100 (100.0)
Professional e.g., MBBS, CA, etc.	18 (30.0)	14 (23.3)	10 (16.7)	18 (30.0)	60 (100.0)
Total	98 (27.9)	76 (21.7)	65 (18.5)	112 (31.9)	351 (100.0)

Note: Figures in parentheses represent the percentages

It can be seen from the table reveals that when initiators are less educated i.e., up to class XII, more time is taken by the families to purchase the product as compared to households where initiators are better educated. chi-square does not show a significant relationship between education and time taken to purchase a product.

Time Taken vis-à-vis Sex of Initiators

It was decided to see if there is a significant difference in the time taken in the purchase of a durable when the initiators are male or female. The cross tabulation between time taken vis-à-vis sex is shown in Table 4.9.

Table 4.9: Time Taken vis-à-vis Sex of Initiators

Sex	Actual Time Taken				
	<=2 Weeks	2 Weeks – 1 Month	1 - 2 Months	> 2 Months	Total
Male	38 (26.0)	31 (21.2)	31 (21.2)	46 (31.5)	146 (100.0)
Female	60 (29.3)	45 (22.0)	34 (16.6)	66 (32.2)	205 (100.0)
Total	98 (27.9)	76 (21.7)	65 (18.5)	112 (31.9)	351 (100.0)

Note: Figures in parentheses represent the percentages

It can be seen from the table that there is no difference in the amount of time taken in the purchase of a durable with relation to the sex of initiating members. chi-square does not show a significant relationship between sex and time taken to purchase a product.

Time Taken vis-à-vis Occupation of Initiators

The cross tabulation was done to see if there is a significant difference in the time taken in the purchase of a durable with initiating members' occupation. This is shown in Table 4.10.

It can be seen that the time taken to purchase the product varies with the occupation of the initiators. chi-square value, which is significant at 0.01 level shows that the time taken to purchase the product differs significantly with the occupation of the initiator.

In cases where the initiators are students or housewives or are in government service the families have been found to take relatively more time to purchase the product as compared to the initiators in other occupations. This could be a

Table 4.10: Time Taken in Purchase Decision vis-à-vis Occupation

Occupation	Average Time Taken to Purchase (months)	Actual Time Taken				
		<= 2 Weeks	2 Weeks – 1 Month	1 - 2 Months	> 2 Months	Total
Government Servant	1.51	17 (33.3)	6 (11.8)	6 (11.8)	22 (43.1)	51 (100.0)
Own Business	1.28	12 (20.7)	17 (29.3)	17 (29.3)	12 (20.7)	58 (100.0)
Housewife	1.42	24 (29.6)	17 (21.0)	10 (12.3)	30 (37.0)	81 (100.0)
Student	1.42	28 (28.0)	18 (18.0)	20 (20.0)	34 (34.0)	100 (100.0)
Others #	1.23	17 (27.9)	18 (29.5)	12 (19.7)	14 (23.0)	61 (100.0)
Total		98 (27.9)	76 (21.7)	65 (18.5)	112 (31.9)	351 (100.0)
		chi-square = 20.9**				

**Significant at 0.01 level

Note: Figures in parentheses represent the percentages

#Others include retired persons and people working in private concern.

reflection on the ability to contribute financially in the purchase of the consumer durable product.

Time Taken vis-à-vis Family Size

In order to see if the time taken in the purchase of a consumer durable product varies with the family size cross tabulation between the two variables was done. This is shown in Table 4.11.

It can be noted from the table that there is no difference in time taken in the purchase decision with relation to family size. Thus, family size does not affect the amount of time taken to purchase the product. chi-square test does not show a significant relationship between family size and time taken to purchase a product.

Table 4.11: Time Taken vis-à-vis Family Size

Family Size	Actual Time Taken				
	<= 2 Weeks	2 Weeks – 1 Month	1 - 2 Months	> 2 Months	Total
Two	14 (32.6)	9 (20.9)	9 (20.9)	11 (25.6)	43 (100.0)
Three	23 (30.7)	13 (17.3)	18 (24.0)	21 (28.0)	75 (100.0)
Four	28 (23.0)	29 (23.8)	17 (13.9)	48 (39.3)	122 (100.0)
Five	24 (32.9)	17 (23.3)	9 (12.3)	23 (31.5)	73 (100.0)
> Six	9 (23.7)	8 (21.1)	12 (31.6)	9 (23.7)	38 (100.0)
Total	98 (27.9)	76 (21.7)	65 (18.5)	112 (31.9)	351 (100.0)

Note: Figures in parentheses represent the percentages

Time Taken vis-à-vis Product Purchased

Since we have considered six different types of products in our study it was decided to see whether the time taken to purchase varies with the products. A cross tabulation between time taken to purchase and the products is shown in Table 4.12.

Table 4.12: Time Taken in Purchase Decision vis-à-vis Product

Product Purchased	Actual Time Taken		
	< = One Month	> One Month	Total
Audio System	34 (56.7)	26 (43.3)	56 (100.0)
Car	16 (27.1)	43 (72.9)	59 (100.0)
Personal Computer	18 (35.3)	33 (64.7)	51 (100.0)
Refrigerator	27 (45.0)	33 (55.0)	60 (100.0)
Television	38 (64.4)	21 (35.6)	59 (100.0)
Washing Machine	41 (66.1)	21 (33.9)	62 (100.0)
Total	174 (49.6)	177 (50.4)	351 (100.0)
Chi-square = 29.76**			

** Significant at 0.01 level

Note: Figures in parentheses represent the percentages

In order to have a fruitful interpretation and to apply the statistical test correctly, it was decided to combine the time spans (less than two weeks and two weeks to one month into one time span viz. less than equal to one month; one month to two months and more than two months into the other time span viz. more than one month) as shown in the Table 4.12.

It is evident from the Table 4.12 that the time taken to purchase a car, personal computer and refrigerator is relatively more than in the case of other products. chi-square value, which is significant at 0.01 level shows that product categories and the time taken to purchase them differ significantly.

Reasons for the Purchase of Product

Following are some of the reasons mentioned by the initiator to its family members as to why the product was necessary. The reasons mentioned by the initiators for the purchase of the product are shown in Table 4.13.

The most important reason for the purchase of a durable is convenience (40.5 percent), followed by replacement due to availability of new products with advanced features (37.3 percent). The next most important reason for purchasing a durable was entertainment (21.9 percent), followed by replacement of old product not functioning properly (19.9 percent). Reasons such as consumer offers, automation and up-gradation of status have been cited by only a few respondents. It can be seen that more initiators wanted to replace their older products to up-grade to new features (37.3 percent) as compared to those who felt that the older products were not functioning properly (19.9 percent).

This has important implications for the marketers as an incentive to constantly upgrade their products and introduce technologically superior features. Reasons such as education and flexibility are apparently not applicable for all the products considered in the study and restricted to personal computers and cars and washing machines respectively.

Table 4.13: Reasons for the Purchase of Product (N=351)

Reasons for purchase	Frequency	Percent
Replacement-old product not functioning properly	70	19.9
Replacement-new products with advanced features	131	37.3
New product with attractive offer	20	5.7
Entertainment	77	21.9
Status symbol	30	8.5
Education	48	13.7
Convenience	142	40.5
Flexibility	61	17.4
Better than doing it manually	28	8.0
Commercial purpose	7	2.0

Note: Multiple Answers

Mentioning Purchased Product's Need in the Past

Initiators were asked whether the need for the product purchased was mentioned in the past also when it was turned down. Responses to this query are listed in the Table 4.14.

It is quite likely that a family may not be able to satisfy some of the needs of members immediately. Needs of different family members are prioritised depending upon the availability of the funds and the utility of the products under consideration. Such needs which could not be considered at a given point are raised again for review after some time.

Table 4.14: Mentioning Purchased Product's Need in the Past

Need Mentioned in the Past	Frequency	Percent
Yes	95	27.1
No	256	72.9
Total	351	100.0

The decision to postpone a purchase is not taken unilaterally by any one member, but as we shall see in the following chapters, it is a decision by the family as a whole after the views of various members are taken. It should also be noted that the competition for a consumer durable product in a family does not necessarily come from other consumer durable products only but possibly from clothes, furnishings, a vacation and education etc. also.

Almost 27 percent of the initiators' request for purchase was turned down in the past. This has important implications for the marketer of consumer durable products where the sale of their products is getting postponed. It is a challenge for them to see how they can ensure that these 27 percent of the total cases are not postponed and their own brands only are selected.

Further, it is important to understand the reasons due to which the requests of the initiators could not be entertained in the past. This is discussed in the next topic.

Reasons for Postponing the Purchase of Product

Initiators whose request in the past for the product was turned down were asked to cite the reasons for postponement. The reasons mentioned by the initiators as to why the product was not purchased earlier are shown in Table 4.15.

Table 4.15: Reasons for Postponing the Purchase of Product (N=95)

Reasons	Frequency	Percent
Insufficient funds in the past	39	41.1
One or the other family members didn't agree with the utility of the product	24	25.2
Other products were given preference	9	9.5
Need felt was not so strong	28	29.5
Wanted to wait for new features	4	4.2
Old product still functional	16	16.8

Note: Multiple Answers

Insufficient funds has been cited by 41.1 percent of the initiators as the reason for postponing the purchase. This means that the family members were agreeable to the product under consideration as far as the utility of the product was concerned but the family did not have sufficient funds to purchase the products then. This condition is different from the one where 'the need felt was not so strong' (mentioned by 29.5 percent initiators) or 'one or the other members did not agree with the utility of the product' (mentioned by 25.2 percent initiators). In both these cases either the initiating member himself or other members are not sure about the utility of the product. Funds are not a constraint in this case. An example could be the proposal by a child to purchase a personal computer to which the parents are not convinced.

In only 9.5 percent cases other products were actually purchased instead. This could mean that of the 27 percent cases where the sale is actually postponed, in only 10 percent cases other products are actually purchased. This means that the sale in 90 percent of the total postponed cases the purchase is simply shifted to a later date. One of the important reason for postponement refers to the case of replacement of the old product. In 16.8 percent cases the older product was felt to be performing well enough, not warranting a replacement. Only 4.2 percent of the initiators with postponed cases waited for better features to be available in the products.

Need Specified for the Purchase of Product in Terms of Type, Features and Functions

Initiators were asked to mention if they had specified the need in terms of type, features and functions. Results to the above statement are shown in Table 4.16.

Table 4.16: Need specified for the Purchase of Product in Terms of Type, Features and Functions

Need Specified In Terms Of Type, Features And Functions	Frequency	Percent
Yes	320	91.2
No	31	8.8
Total	351	100.0

It is clear from the Table 4.16 that most of the initiators (91.2 percent) are reasonably clear about the features of the product they wish to purchase. This could mean that before initiating the process, the members had personally dwelled over the product and were reasonable clear as to what they wanted. In the subsequent topic where the satisfaction level of these initiators is gauged, we shall understand how much the specifications of the purchased product vary from those of the initiators.

Extent of Satisfaction from the Purchased Product

All those initiators 320 (91.2 percent) who said that they had defined their need in terms of type, features, etc., were asked to specify how satisfied they were now with the actual purchase. The extent to which the initiator was satisfied from the purchased product is shown in Table 4.17.

Table 4.17: Extent of Satisfaction from the Purchased Product (N= 320)

Extent Of Satisfaction From The Purchased Product	Frequency	Percent
Somewhat Satisfied	130	40.1
Completely Satisfied	190	59.4

From these initiators, as high as 40.1 percent were only somewhat satisfied with the purchase. This could mean that the influences of other members actually changed the specification of the purchased product. It is expected that different members of the family are likely to impose their views and preferences on a product that is common to all of them. 59.4 percent initiators were completely satisfied so their expectations were fully met or even exceeded.

At this stage it was decided to see whether there was a difference in the time taken to purchase with the level of satisfaction experienced by the initiators. For this purpose, the means, the standard deviations and the t-values with reference to the extent of satisfaction by the initiators from the purchased product were computed. The time taken to purchase a durable product when the initiator mentioned the need is shown in Table 4.18. Initiators were further categorised as those whose need was 'completely met' and those whose need was 'somewhat met' from the purchased product.

Table 4.18: Time Taken in Purchase Decision *vis-à-vis* Level of Needs Met

Need	N	Mean	Standard Deviation	t-Value
Somewhat Met	130	2.70	1.11	2.12*
Completely Met	190	2.41	1.26	

*Significant at 0.05 level

The t-value in the above Table depicts that respondents belonging to the category of 'somewhat met need' are significantly different from the respondents of the category of 'completely met need' in the time taken to purchase the products. The mean value shows that the respondents of 'somewhat met need' take more time to purchase a durable product as compared to the respondents with 'completely met needs'.

Conclusion

The initiator member is the one who starts the process in the family which ultimately leads to the purchase of the consumer durable product. The initiator is typically a young female member who is likely to be either the housewife or one of the children in the family. Need for audio system, personal computer and television is likely to be first expressed by the children in the family whereas the wife is more likely to initiate the process for the purchase of a refrigerator and washing machine. Husband has turned out to be the initiating member for the purchase of car. In the family, initiators had expressed their need for the product to the husband, which shows that the husband is expected to play an important role in the final purchase. Average time taken in the purchase of a consumer durable product in a family is around six weeks that further depends on the monthly household income and the price of the product. Further, the time taken to purchase also depends upon the age of the initiating member and the type of product purchased. The most important reasons cited for the purchase of a product are convenience and replacement of the old product because of availability of a new product with advanced features. Around one in four initiators had expressed the need for the same product in the past also when it was not considered in the family. The purchase was postponed primarily because of insufficient funds. Another reason for postponement was that the family felt that the need for the product was not so strong at that point of time. Most of the initiators expressed their need for the product in detail, specifying the type, features and functions however, only sixty percent felt that their needs were fully met from the purchased product. This signifies that specifications of the product given by the initiator are likely to change during the decision-making process due to family dynamics involving requirements of other members and financial constraints.

5

Buying Roles: The Influencer

In the context of the buying decision, the influencer is a person whose views or advice carry some weight in the final decision. Family members acting as influencers can affect purchasing decision in many ways. Broadly, in the case of a family making a purchase decision, members acting as influencers express their views regarding the features available in a particular product and the brand to be selected. The family buying process is quite similar to the organisational buying process in that in both of them, there are several persons/departments including specialists in each of their areas of operation, who influence the purchasing decision. In the case of a family, however, the influencers do not have any expertise but assume their respective roles on the basis of the family dynamics. The influencers either take up the role voluntarily or are assigned it by another member.

The role of an influencer spans across stages II and III (information search and evaluation of alternatives) of the decision-making process.

Need Recognition →	Information Search →	Evaluation of Alternatives →	Purchase Decision →	Post-purchase Behaviour
INITIATORS				
	INFLUENCERS			

The purchase of a consumer durable product in a family invariably affects all the members. Once it has been announced in the family that a particular consumer durable product is going to be purchased, different members start providing whatever information is available to them on the product. At times, some members may even be assigned the task of gathering certain information about the product. For collecting additional data, the influencers may any of the four basic sources of information, viz. personal, commercial, public and experiential. The degree of acceptance of the information and the preferences of the influencers may, however, vary. It is important to understand to what extent these suggestions are or can be considered. Although there is a separate role called 'decider', the degree of consideration of the ideas and suggestions depends upon all the members who are acting as influencers. The person whom the influencers confide in assumes the role of the moderator. The same person may also instruct the members to collect the desired information.

Characteristics of the Influencer

The demographic characteristics of influencers are shown in Table 5.1. In total there are 468 influencers.

Unlike in the case of initiators there is no fixed profile emerging in the case of influencers. There seems to be a uniform spread across all the characteristics except that there seems to be more numbers of students (22.9 percent) and youngsters (32.9 percent influencers are below 25 years of age) who have acted as influencers. 86.1 percent of the influencers have done their graduation or higher level of studies.

There are 468 members in 313 families who have acted as influencers which means that more than one members in certain families have acted as influencers.

Table 5.1:Characteristics of the Influencer (Respondents)

Characteristics	Frequency	Percent
SEX		
Male	249	53.2
Female	219	46.8
AGE		
Less than 18 years	42	9
19-25 years	112	23.9
26-35 years	139	29.7
36-50 years	113	24.1
More than 50 years	62	13.2
EDUCATION		
<= XII	65	13.9
Graduate	181	38.7
Post Graduate	133	28.4
Professional e.g., MBBS,	89	19
OCCUPATION		
Government Service	85	18.2
Own Business	56	12
Self Employed Professional	40	8.5
Working in Pvt. Concern	74	15.8
Retired	13	2.8
Housewife	93	19.9
Student	107	22.9

Member-wise Status of Influencers

Out of a total of 468 influencers Table 5.2 shows the member-wise status of influencers.

As is clear from Table 5.2 that out of a total of 468 influencers the maximum number of influencers are children at 160, i.e., 34.18 percent. 140 (29.9 percent) husbands and 137 (29.3 percent) wives have acted as influencers. Grand parents have acted as influencers in 18 cases i.e. in 3.9 percent of cases.

Table 5.2: Member-wise Status of Influencers

Member	Frequency	Percent
Husband	140	29.9
Wife	137	29.3
Child 1	120	25.6
Child 2	38	8.1
Child 3	2	0.4
Grand father	11	2.4
Grand mother	7	1.5
Member A	11	2.4
Member B	2	0.4
Total	468	100.0

Influencer Member vis-à-vis the Product Purchased

A cross-tabulation was made between the influencer member and the product purchased by the family. This is shown in Table 5.3.

It is clear from the table that as the durable product changes different family members become more active as influencers. In the case of personal computer children and others have acted as influencers in maximum cases. Children have also acted as important influencers in the purchase of audio system and television. The Wife has acted as strong influencers in the purchase of all durable products except personal computer. The husband has been the influencer in all the durable products with almost equal frequency.

Table 5.3: Influencer Member vis-à-vis Product Purchased

Product Purchased	No. of Influencer Members			
	Husband	Wife	Children and others #	Total
Audio System	22 (27.2)	24 (29.6)	35 (43.2)	81 (100.0)
Car	25 (32.5)	27 (35.1)	25 (32.5)	77 (100.0)
Personal Computer	15 (27.3)	5 (9.1)	35 (63.6)	55 (100.0)
Refrigerator	28 (31.5)	27 (30.3)	34 (38.2)	89 (100.0)
Television	20 (28.2)	21 (29.6)	30 (42.2)	71 (100.0)
Washing Machine	30 (31.6)	33 (34.7)	32 (33.7)	95 (100.0)
Total	140 (29.9)	137 (29.3)	191 (40.8)	468 (100.0)
chi-square = 20.1*				

*Significant at 0.05 level.
Note: Figures in parentheses represent the percentages.
#'Others' represent grand parents etc. whose frequency is taken along with 'children'.

Suggestions for Technical Aspects of the Product

Influencers were asked if they had mentioned certain technical aspects to be considered while selecting the product. Response to this statement is shown in Table 5.4.

Table 5.4: Suggestions for Technical Aspects of the Product

Suggestions For Technical Aspects	Frequency	Percent
Yes	413	88.2
No	55	11.8
Total	468	100.0

Members acting as influencers are expected to have provided certain technical inputs which would have helped in selecting from various models available of the product. Out of 468 influencers, a large number 413 (88.2 percent) made suggestions on the technical aspects about the product under consideration.

It was decided to study what impact different family and personal characteristics of the influencers had on the contribution from the influencers on the technical aspects of the product under consideration. It can be of interest to know whether certain types of family members are more active influencers than others. Cross tabulations were made between the family (and personal) characteristics of the influencers and whether they made any technical contribution in the decision-making process.

Income and the Suggestions for Technical Aspects

A cross tabulation between the monthly household income and the technical suggestions made by the influencer with regard to the product are shown in Table 5.5.

From Table 5.5 it can be clearly seen that there is no difference in the income of the influencer and the suggestions regarding technical aspects. chi-square test also does not report a significant difference with respect to monthly household income and suggestions made by the influencer with regard to technical aspects.

Table 5.5: Income and the Suggestions for Technical Aspects

Monthly Household Income (Rs.)	Suggestions for technical aspects		
	Yes	No	Total
<= 10,000	46 (82.1)	10 (17.9)	56 (100.0)
10,001-15,000	85 (93.4)	6 (6.6)	91 (100.0)
15,001-20,000	111 (86.7)	17 (13.3)	128 (100.0)
20,001-25,000	64 (91.4)	6 (8.6)	70 (100.0)
> 25,000	107 (87.0)	16 (13.0)	123 (100.0)
Total	413 (88.2)	55 (11.8)	468 (100.0)

Note: Figures in parentheses represent the percentages

Age and the Suggestions for Technical Aspects

A cross tabulation with the age of the influencer and the technical suggestions made by him with regard to the durable product are shown in Table 5.6.

From the table it can be seen that there is only a very small difference in the age groups of the influencer and the suggestions regarding technical aspects. A relatively smaller proportion of the influencers in the age group of eighteen or

Table 5.6: Age and the Suggestions for Technical Aspects

Age	Suggestions for technical aspects		
	Yes	No	Total
< =18 years	34 (81.0)	8 (19.0)	42 (100.0)
19-25 years	97 (86.6)	15 (13.4)	112 (100.0)
26-35 years	126 (90.6)	13 (9.4)	139 (100.0)
36-50 years	102 (90.3)	11 (9.7)	113 (24.1)
> 50 years	54 (87.1)	8 (12.9)	62 (13.2)
Total	413 (88.2)	55 (11.8)	468 (100.0)

Note: Figures in parentheses represent the percentages

less has made technical suggestions about the product. chi-square test also does not report a significant difference with respect to age of the influencer and suggestions made by him regarding technical aspects.

Education and the Suggestions for Technical Aspects

A cross tabulation with the educational level of the influencer and the technical suggestions made by him is shown in Table 5.7.

It is clear from the table, as the education of the influencer increases they are more likely to give technical suggestions. chi-square value significant at 0.01 level shows a significant difference between level of education and the technical suggestions made.

Table 5.7: Education and the Suggestions for Technical Aspects

Education	Suggestions for technical aspects		
	Yes	No	Total
XII and below	49 (75.4)	16 (24.6)	65 (100.0)
Graduate	159 (87.8)	22 (12.2)	181 (100.0)
Post-Graduate	121 (91.0)	12 (9.0)	133 (100.0)
Professional	84 (94.4)	5 (5.6)	89 (100.0)
Total	413 (88.2)	55 (11.8)	468 (100.0)
Chi-square = 14.6**			

** Significant at 0.01 level.
Note: Figures in parentheses represent the percentages.

Sex and the Suggestions for Technical Aspects

A cross tabulation with the sex of the influencer and the technical suggestions made by him with regard to the purchase of a consumer durable product is shown in Table 5.8.

It is clear from the table that male members in the role of influencer are more likely to contribute on the technical aspects of the consumer durable product to be purchased rather than the female members. chi-square value significant at 0.01 level shows a significant difference between sex and the suggestions made with regard to technical aspects of the durable product.

Occupation and the Suggestions for Technical Aspects

A cross tabulation with the occupation of the influencer and the technical suggestions made by him with regard to the durable product are shown in Table 5.9.

Table 5.8: Sex and the Suggestions for Technical Aspects

Sex	Suggestions for technical aspects		
	Yes	No	Total
Male	234 (94.0)	15 (6.0)	249 (100.0)
Female	179 (81.7)	40 (18.3)	219 (100.0)
Total	413 (88.2)	55 (11.8)	468 (100.0)
Chi-square = 15.7**			

** Significant at 0.01 level.
Note: Figures in parentheses represent the percentages.

It can be deduced from the table that a relatively smaller proportion of the housewives and students as influencers are likely to give technical suggestions as compared to the members with government service, own businessmen, professionals and retired persons who are categorised as others in the Table 5.9. chi-square test shows a significant difference between occupation and suggestions regarding technical aspects.

Family Size and the Suggestions For Technical Aspects

A cross tabulation with the family size and the technical suggestions made by the influencer with regard to the purchase of a consumer durable product is shown in Table 5.10. It is clear from the table that there is no significant difference amongst the family size for the suggestions made by the influencer with regard to technical aspects. chi-square test does not show a significant difference between family size and suggestions regarding technical aspects.

Table 5.9: Occupation and Suggestions for Technical Aspects

Occupation	Suggestions for technical aspects		
	Yes	No	Total
Government Servant	79 (92.9)	6 (7.1)	85 (100.0)
Own Business	90 (93.7)	6 (6.3)	96 (100.0)
Housewife	72 (77.4)	5 (5.7)	87 (100.0)
Student	90 (84.1)	21 (22.6)	93 (100.0)
Others#	82 (94.3)	17 (15.9)	107 (100.0)
Total	413 (88.2)	55 (11.8)	468 (100.0)
Chi-square = 19.9**			

** Significant at 0.01 level.
Note: Figures in parentheses represent the percentages.
Others include professionals and retired persons.

Table 5.10: Family Size and Suggestions for Technical Aspects

Family Size	Suggestions for technical aspects		
	Yes	No	Total
Two	50 (94.3)	3 (5.7)	53 (100.0)
Three	92 (90.2)	10 (9.8)	102 (100.0)
Four	138 (85.2)	24 (14.8)	162 (100.0)
Five	89 (91.8)	8 (8.2)	97 (100.0)
> Six	44 (81.5)	10 (18.5)	54 (100.0)
Total	413 (88.2)	55 (11.8)	468 (100.0)

Product and the Suggestions for Technical Aspects

A cross tabulation with the consumer durable product and the technical suggestions made by the influencers is shown in Table 5.11.

Table 5.11: Product and Suggestions for Technical Aspects

Product	Suggestions for technical aspects		
	Yes	No	Total
Audio System	69 (85.2)	12 (14.8)	81 (100.0)
Car	65 (84.4)	12 (15.6)	77 (100.0)
Personal Computer	49 (89.1)	6 (10.9)	55 (100.0)
Refrigerator	83 (93.3)	6 (10.9)	89 (100.0)
Television	61 (85.9)	10 (14.1)	71 (100.0)
Washing Machine	86 (90.5)	9 (9.5)	95 (100.0)
Total	413 (88.2)	55 (11.8)	468 (100.0)

Note: Figures in parentheses represent the percentages.

It is clear from the table that there is no significant difference amongst the various product categories and the suggestions made by the influencer with regard to technical aspects. Amongst the product categories the influencers of refrigerator have given the maximum technical suggestions. chi-square test does not show a significant difference between product categories and suggestions regarding technical aspects.

Technical Factors Considered by the Influencers

All the 413 (88.2 percent) influencers who said that they had suggested certain technical aspects to be taken into consideration while selecting the product were further asked to list the factors which they considered important. Some of the factors, which the influencer found to be most important are shown in Table 5.12.

Table 5.12: Technical Aspects Considered (N=413)

Technical Aspects	Frequency	Percent
Features	303	73.4
Quality	300	72.6
Performance	322	80
Ease of operation	138	33.4
Aesthetics	95	23.0
After-sales service	169	40.9
Any other	18	4.4

Note: Multiple Answers

The influencer members were further asked to mention specific technical aspects that are discussed as follows. The three most important technical aspects considered by influencers for the purchase are performance, mentioned by 322 (80 percent) respondents, features, by 303 (73.4 percent) and quality by 300 (72.6 percent).

Ease of operation and after sales service as parts of specifications were mentioned by relatively lesser number of influencer members at 33.4 and 40.9 percent respectively. After sales service may not be an immediate concern of many at the time of purchase. Interestingly, aesthetics were covered by only 23 percent of the influencer members in their specifications. It can possibly be explained by the fact that aesthetics are quite difficult to specify and might be limited to comparison of various models on their looks from the catalogues. It will be a factor at the back of the mind when certain models would have been selected. These revelations are an important input for the marketers of consumer durable products.

Extent of Consideration of Influencers' Suggestions

All the 413 (88.2 percent) influencers were asked to rate how far the various technical suggestions made by them were considered in the final purchase. The rating given by influencer is shown in Table 5.13

Table 5.13: Extent of Consideration of Influencers' Suggestions

Influencers Rating	Frequency	Percent
Somewhat Considered	172	41.6
Completely Considered	241	58.4
Total	413	100.0

Based on pre-testing of the questionnaire, it was decided to use a two-point scale in place of the five-point scale used in other places, since the frequency of responses in other sets was quite insignificant. As can be seen from the table 241 (58.4 percent) of influencers felt that the suggestions made by them were completely considered in the product purchased whereas 172 (41.6 percent) influencers said that the suggestions made by them were only somewhat considered. These responses of the influencers when seen along with the responses of the initiators on a similar question (Table 4.17) leads to important findings. In case of both initiators and influencers, only around 60 percent (59.4 percent initiators and 58.4 percent influencers) felt that their specifications were fully considered whereas around 40 percent in both the cases felt that their specifications were only somewhat considered. This means there are compromises by all the members in the family when it comes to the purchase decision for consumer durable products and the proportion of the satisfied members is quite similar in both the groups.

We shall now see if certain demographic characteristics of the influencer members and that of the family have an impact on the extent the influencers' suggestions on technical aspects, which were further, considered in the purchased product.

Income and the Extent of Consideration of Influencers' Suggestions

A cross tabulation between monthly household income and the extent of consideration of influencers' suggestions is shown in Table 5.14.

From Table 5.14 it can be clearly seen that there is no difference in the income of the influencer and the extent of consideration of influencers' suggestions. chi-square test also does not report a significant difference.

Table 5.14: Income and the Extent of Consideration of Influencers' Suggestions

Monthly Household Income (Rs.)	Extent of Consideration of Influencers' Suggestions		
	Somewhat Met	Completely Met	Total
< 10,000	21(45.7)	25 (54.3)	46 (100.0)
10,001-15,000	25 (29.4)	60 (70.6)	85 (100.0)
15,001-20,000	46 (41.4)	65 (58.6)	111 (100.0)
20,001-25,000	33 (51.6)	31(48.4)	64 (100.0)
> 25,000	47 (43.9)	60 (56.1)	107 (100.0)
Total	172 (41.7)	241 (58.3)	413 (100.0)

Note: Figures in parentheses represent the percentages

Age and the Extent of Consideration of Influencers' Suggestions

A cross tabulation with the age of the influencer and the extent of consideration of influencers' suggestions are shown in Table 5.15.

From Table 5.15 it can be clearly seen that with the increase in age of the proportion of the influencers whose technical suggestions have been completely considered in the purchased product has increased. Cases where the suggestions made by influencers aged up-to twenty-five years old were completely considered were found to be in relatively lesser numbers. This can be interpreted that in the Indian families views of younger people are accepted to a relatively lesser extent. chi-square test shows a significant difference between age of the influencer and the consideration of the technical suggestions made by them.

Table 5.15: Age and the Extent of Consideration of Influencers' Suggestions

Age	Extent of Consideration of Influencers' Suggestions		
	Somewhat Met	Completely Met	Total
<=18 years	19 (55.9)	15 (44.1)	34 (100.0)
19-25 years	51 (52.6)	46 (47.4)	97 (100.0)
26-35 years	45 (35.7)	81 (64.3)	126 (100.0)
36-50 years	41 (40.2)	61 (59.8)	102 (100.0)
> 50 years	16 (29.6)	38 (70.4)	54 (100.0)
Total	172 (41.6)	241 (58.4)	413 (100.0)
chi-square = 12.7**			

**Significant at 0.01 level.
Note: Figures in parentheses represent the percentages

Education and the Extent of Consideration of Influencers' Suggestions

A cross tabulation with the education of the influencer and the extent of consideration of influencers' suggestions is shown in Table 5.16.

As can be seen from the table, education of the influencer does not have an impact on the extent of consideration of influencers' suggestions. chi-square test also does not show a significant difference.

Table 5.16: Education and the Extent of Consideration of Influencers' Suggestions

Education	**Extent of Consideration of Influencers' Suggestions**		
	Somewhat Met	Completely Met	Total
XII and below	22 (44.9)	27 (55.1)	49 (100.0)
Graduate	66 941.5)	93 (58.5)	159 (100.0)
Post-Graduate	53 (43.8)	68 (56.2)	121 (100.0)
Professional	31 (36.9)	53 (63.1)	84 (100.0)
Total	172 (41.6)	241 (58.4)	413 (100.0)

Note: Figures in parentheses represent the percentages.

Sex and the Extent of Consideration of Influencers' Suggestions

A cross tabulation between the sex of the influencer and the extent of consideration of influencers' suggestions is given in Table 5.17.

Table 5.17: Sex and the Extent of Consideration of Influencers' Suggestions

Sex	**Extent of Consideration of Influencers' Suggestions**		
	Somewhat Met	Completely Met	Total
Male	95 (40.6)	139 (59.4)	234 (100.0)
Female	77 (43.0)	102 (57.0)	179 (100.0)
Total	172 (41.7)	241 (58.3)	413 (100.0)

Note: Figures in parentheses represent the percentages.

As is shown from the table that there is not much difference whether the influencer member was a male or a female as far as the consideration of the technical suggestions in the purchase decision is concerned.

Occupation and the Extent of Consideration of Influencers' Suggestions

A cross tabulation with the occupation of the influencer and the extent of consideration of influencers' suggestions is shown in Table 5.18.

Table 5.18: Occupation and the Extent of Consideration of Influencers' Suggestions

Occupation	Extent of Consideration of Influencers' Suggestions		
	Somewhat Met	Completely Met	Total
Government Servant	31 (39.2)	48 (60.8)	79 (100.0)
Own Business	20 (38.5)	32 (61.5)	52 (100.0)
Self Employed Professional	10 (26.3)	28 (73.7)	38 (100.0)
Housewife	31 (43.1)	41 (56.9)	72 (100.0)
Student	49 (54.4)	41 (45.6)	90 (100.0)
Others#	31 (37.8)	51 (62.2)	82 (100.0)
Total	172 (41.7)	241 (58.3)	413 (100.0)
chi-square = 10.7*			

** Significant at 0.05 level.

Note: Figures in parentheses represent the percentages.

Others include working in private concern and retired persons.

It is clear from the table that the students feel that their technical suggestions have been considered to a relatively lesser extent as compared to the housewives, government servants, businessmen, professionals and retired persons. chi-square test also shows a significant difference between the influencers occupation and the extent of Consideration of their suggestions in the purchased product.

Family Size and the Extent of Consideration of Influencers' Suggestions

A cross tabulation with the family size and the extent of consideration of influencers' suggestions is shown in Table 5.19.

Table 5.19: Family Size and the Extent of Consideration of Influencers' Suggestions

Family Size	Extent of Consideration of Influencers' Suggestions		
	Somewhat Met	Completely Met	Total
Two	24 (48.0)	26 (52.0)	50 (100.0)
Three	40 (43.5)	52 (56.5)	92 (100.0)
Four	62 (44.9)	76 (55.1)	138 (100.0)
Five	34 (38.2)	55 (61.8)	89 (100.0)
> Six	12 (27.3)	32 (72.7)	44 (100.0)
Total	172 (41.6)	241 (58.4)	413 (100.0)

Note: Figures in parentheses represent the percentages.

It is clear from the table that as the family size changes there is not much difference in the extent of consideration of the influencers' views. A larger proportion of the influencers belonging to family size of six or more members feels that their suggestions have been considered in the final purchase. chi-square test does not show a significant difference between family size and the consideration of suggestions made by the influencers in the final purchase.

Product and the Extent of Consideration of Influencers' Suggestions

A cross tabulation with and the extent of consideration of influencers' suggestions with various product categories is shown in Table 5.20.

It is clear from the table that the television influencers have been found to be most satisfied with the consideration of suggestions made by them in the final purchase with regard to technical aspects. This is being followed by the influencers of washing machine and audio system who have been found to be satisfied as compared to other product categories in the consideration of the suggestions made by them in the final purchase. chi-square test reveals a significant difference on account of different durable products and the influencers' suggestions being considered in the final purchase.

Brand Preference of the Influencers

Influencers were asked whether they advised for or against any brands. Responses to this question are given in Table 5.21.

Table 5.20: Product and the Extent of Consideration of Influencers' Suggestions

Product	Extent of Consideration of Influencers' Suggestions		
	Somewhat Met	Completely Met	Total
Audio System	25 (36.2)	44 (63.8)	69 (100.0)
Car	38 (58.5)	27 (41.5)	65 (100.0)
Personal Computer	26 (53.1)	23 (46.9)	49 (100.0)
Refrigerator	37 (44.6)	46 (55.4)	83 (100.0)
Television	16 (26.2)	45 (73.8)	61 (100.0)
Washing Machine	30 (34.9)	56 (65.1)	86 (100.0)
Total	172 (41.7)	241 (58.3)	413 (100.0)
chi-square = 18.9**			

**Significant at 0.01 level.
Note: Figures in parentheses represent the percentages.

Table 5.21: Brand Preference of the Influencers

Brand Preference	Frequency	Percent
Yes	310	66.2
No	158	33.8
Total	468	100.0

A majority of the respondents, 310 out of 468 (66.2 percent) had expressed their views for the brands to be preferred or not. In a family, members are likely to have their own preferences for different brands for a given product. The perception regarding brands can be formed from their own earlier experience or any of the external factors such as advertisements, reviews, word of mouth etc. Each of the influencer members is going to list the merits and demerits of the brands and after a detailed evaluation brands are going to be selected or rejected. It is possible that members may try to corroborate their claims regarding the brands by gathering information from various sources. This aspect has far reaching implications for the marketer who has to ensure that his brand is first in the awareness set and finally reaches in the choice set and is finally purchased. However we have also seen that not all the influencer members have made their suggestions regarding the brands. We shall now see if there is any relationship between the personal or family characteristics and the contribution made regarding the brands in a family purchase situation for consumer durable products.

Following tables show cross tabulations between different variables and influencers' contribution with suggestions regarding brands.

Income and the Suggestions for Brands

A cross tabulation of the influencers monthly household income and contribution regarding suggestions for brands is shown in Table 5.22.

From Table 5.22 it can be seen that there is no significant difference in monthly household income and contribution regarding suggestions for brands. chi-square test also does not report a significant difference.

Table 5.22: Income and the Suggestions for Brands

Monthly Household	Suggestions for Brands		
	Yes	No	Total
<= 10,000	36 (64.3)	20 (35.7)	56 (100.0)
10,001-15,000	60 (65.9)	31 (34.1)	91 (100.0)
15,001-20,000	84 (65.6)	44 (34.4)	128 (100.0)
20,001-25,000	49 (70.0)	21 (30.0)	70 (100.0)
> 25,000	81 (65.9)	42 (34.1)	123 (100.0)
Total	310 (66.2)	158 (33.8)	468 (100.0)

Age and the Suggestions for Brands

A cross tabulation with age of the influencers and contribution regarding suggestions for brands is shown in Table 5.23.

Table 5.23: Age and the Suggestions for Brands

Age	Suggestions For Brands		
	Yes	No	Total
< 18 years	21 (50.0)	21 (50.0)	42 (100.0)
19-25 years	70 (62.5)	42 (37.5)	112 (100.0)
26-35 years	102 (73.4)	37 (26.6)	139 (100.0)
36-50 years	80 (70.8)	33 (29.2)	113 (100.0)
> 50 years	37 (59.7)	25 (40.3)	62 (100.0)
Total	310 (66.2)	158 (33.8)	468 (100.0)
chi-square = 11.7*			

*Significant at 0.05 level

It can be seen from the table that a relatively larger proportion of the influencers in the age groups of 26-35 years (73.4 percent) and 36-50 years (70.8 percent) made some suggestions regarding the brands while purchasing a consumer durable products. It is interesting to note that when we look at the general characteristics of the influencers (Table 5.1) we see that this age group is also the most active as influencers contributing 53.8 of the total influencers.

A relatively smaller proportion of the influencers in the age groups 19-25 years and more than 50 years (62.5 percent and 59.7 percent respectively) have made their contribution regarding the brand selection. The least contribution has come from the influencer members in the age group of less than 18 years as only 50 percent of them have given their suggestions regarding the brands. chi-square test shows a significant difference between the influencers age and the preference for a branded product.

Although the results to this question are quite similar to the one related to the contribution on the technical aspects (Table 5.6), in the present case, members less than 18 years seem to be even less active. This can be a matter of concern for the marketers that the young family members have relatively lesser concern regarding the consumer durable brands.

Education and the Suggestions for Brands

A cross tabulation with education of the influencers and contribution regarding suggestions for brands is shown in Table 5.24.

The table reveals that as we consider better educated groups of the influencers, a higher proportion seems to be making their contributions regarding the brands. chi-square test shows that there is a significant difference between education and contribution regarding suggestions for brands.

Table 5.24: Education and the Suggestions for Brands

Education	Suggestions For Brands		
	Yes	No	Total
XII and below	31 (47.7)	34 (52.3)	65 (100.0)
Graduate	117 (64.6)	64 (35.4)	181 (100.0)
Post-Graduate	90 (67.7)	43 (32.3)	133 (100.0)
Professional	72 (80.9)	17 (19.1)	89 (100.0)
Total	310 (66.2)	158 (33.8)	468 (100.0)
Chi-square = 18.9**			

** Significant at 0.01 level.
Note: Figures in parentheses represent the percentages

Sex and the Suggestions for Brands

A cross tabulation with. sex of the influencers and the contribution regarding suggestions for brands is shown in Table 5.25.

It is clear from the table that male influencers are more active than female members while making contribution regarding the brands to be considered in the purchase decision of consumer durable products. Comparing with the response to the question whether suggestions were made on the technical aspects (Table 5.8), we see that although the results are similar (that a higher proportion of male members made contributions as compared to female member influencers), female member influencers seem to be much more passive when it comes to the brands. They are however more aware about the features and the technical aspects they want in their consumer durable products. chi-square value showed a significant difference between sex of the influencer and the preference for a branded product.

Table 5.25: Sex and the Suggestions for Brands

Sex	Suggestions for Brands		
	Yes	No	Total
Male	199 (79.9)	50 (20.1)	249 (100.0)
Female	111 (50.7)	108 (49.3)	219 (100.0)
Total	310 (66.2)	158 (33.8)	468 (100.0)
chi-square = 43.2**			

** Significant at 0.01 level.
Note: Figures in parentheses represent the percentages

Occupation and the Suggestions For Brands

A cross tabulation with occupation of the influencers and contribution regarding suggestions for brands is shown in Table 5.26.

It is clear from the table that a relatively smaller proportion of housewives and students as influencers has given suggestions regarding the brands in the purchasing decision of consumer durable products as compared to the government servants, businessman, professionals and retired persons. chi-square test shows a significant difference between occupation and preference for a branded product.

Table 5.26: Occupation and the Suggestions For Brands

Occupation	Suggestions For Brands		
	Yes	No	Total
Government Servant	63 (74.1)	22. (25.9)	85 (100.0)
Own Business	68 (70.8)	28 (29.2)	96 (100.0)
Housewife	49 (52.7)	44 (47.3)	87 (100.0)
Student	62 (57.9)	45 (42.1)	93 (100.0)
Others#	68 (78.2)	19 (21.8)	107 (100.0)
Total	310 (66.2)	158 (33.8)	468 (100.0)
chi-square = 19.8**			

** Significant at 0.01 level,
Note: Figures in parentheses represent the percentages
others denotes professionals and retired persons.

Family Size and the Suggestions for Brands

A cross tabulation between the family size and the contribution regarding suggestions for brands is shown in Table 5.27.

It is clear from the table that there is not much difference in proportion of the influencers who made suggestions regarding the brands with the family size. chi-square test does not show a significant difference between family size and the contribution regarding suggestions for brands.

Table 5.27: Family Size and the Suggestions for Brands

Family Size	Suggestions For Brands		
	Yes	No	Total
Two	39 (73.6)	14 (26.4)	53 (100.0)
Three	68 (66.7)	34 (33.3)	102 (100.0)
Four	103 (63.6)	59 (36.4)	162 (100.0)
Five	65 (67.0)	32 (33.0)	97 (100.0)
> Six	35 (64.8)	19 (35.2)	54 (100.0)
Total	310 (66.2)	158 (33.8)	468 (100.0)

Note: Figures in parentheses represent the percentages.

Product and the Suggestions for Brands

A cross tabulation between the product and the contribution regarding suggestions for brands is shown in Table 5.28.

It is clear from the table that there is not much difference in proportion of the influencers who made suggestions regarding the brands when compared with different product categories. chi-square test does not show a significant difference between product categories and the contribution regarding suggestions for brands.

Table 5.28: Product and the Suggestions for Brands

Product	Suggestions For Brands		
	Yes	No	Total
Audio System	55 (67.9)	26 (32.1)	81 (100.0)
Car	53 (68.8)	24 (31.2)	77 (100.0)
Personal Computer	39 (70.9)	16 (29.1)	55 (100.0)
Refrigerator	59 (66.3)	30 (33.7)	89 (100.0)
Television	49 (69.0)	22 (31.0)	71 (100.0)
Washing Machine	55 (57.9)	40 (42.1)	95 (100.0)
Total	310 (66.2)	158 (33.8)	468 (100.0)

Note: Figures in parentheses represent the percentages.

Reasons for Preferring a Particular Brand

Some of the reasons for preferring a particular brand, as mentioned by the influencers are shown in Table 5.29.

All the 310 (66.2 percent) influencers were further asked to mention the reasons that they felt were important for preferring a particular brand. Reasons cited by the majority of influencers were performance (83.2 percent), quality (82.9 percent) and features (74.8 percent). Reasons next in order are price (62.6 percent) and after sales service (54.2 percent) while ease of operation (30.6 percent) and aesthetics (28.7 percent) were cited by the least number of influencer members. When compared with the factors considered while giving suggestions on the technical aspects (Table 5.12) we can see that a similar pattern is emerging while suggesting the brands also.

Table 5.29: Reasons for Preferring a Particular Brand (N=310)

Reasons	Frequency	Percent
Features	232	74.8
Quality	257	82.9
Performance	258	83.2
Ease of operation	95	30.6
Aesthetics	89	28.7
After sales service	168	54.2
Price	194	62.6
Any other	23	7.4

Consideration of Influecers' Brand Preference

We shall now find out whether the suggestions made by the influencer members regarding the brands were considered. It is possible that the influencer members gave two sets of brands, one from which the brands are to be totally avoided and the other to select the brands from, with an order of performance attached. We shall see if the personal and the family characteristics have any impact on the extent of consideration of the suggestions made regarding the brands.

The extent of consideration of the suggestions made by the influencer members regarding the brands is shown in Table 5.30.

The Table 5.30 depicts the extent to which the views of the influencer with regard to the preference for any brand were considered in the final purchase. A cross tabulation has been done with various family characteristics and product categories in order to find out if there is a significant difference with respect to different age groups, change in monthly household income, etc.

Table 5.30: Extent to Which Preference for any Brand was Considered

Rating Scale	Frequency	Percent
Completely Considered	180	58.1
Somewhat Considered	130	41.9
Total	310	100.0

Income and the Extent to which Suggestions for any Brand were Considered

A cross tabulation is done taking the monthly household income and the extent of consideration of the suggestions regarding the brands, which is shown in Table 5.31.

The Table 5.31 depicts that the influencers having the monthly household income up to 15,000 have been found to be more satisfied with the consideration of the views with regard to the brand. Influencers belonging to higher income bracket have not been found to be as satisfied with the consideration of the views with regard to brand. chi-square test also revealed a significant difference between the influencers monthly household income and extent to which views with regard to brand were considered.

Table 5.31: Income and the Extent to which Suggestions for any Brand were Considered

Monthly Household Income (Rs.)	Extent of Consideration of Suggestions for Brands		
	Somewhat Considered	Totally Considered	Total
<= 10,000	10 (27.8)	26 (72.2)	36 (100.0)
10,001-15,000	19 (32.2)	40 (67.8)	59 (100.0)
15,001-20,000	38 (45.2)	46 (54.8)	84 (100.0)
20,001-25,000	27 (55.1)	22 (44.9)	49 (100.0)
> 25,000	36 (43.9)	46 (56.1)	82 (100.0)
Total	130 (41.9)	180 (58.1)	310 (100.0)
Chi-square = 9.2*			

Significant at 0.05 level
Note: Figures in parentheses represent the percentages.

Age and the Extent to which Suggestions for any Brand were Considered

A cross tabulation with age of the influencers and the extent to which preference with regard to brands is considered is given in Table 5.32.

The table reveals that the influencers in the age group of more than fifty years have been found to be more satisfied with the Consideration of views with regard to the brand as compared to others. chi-square test however does not show a significant difference between age of the influencer and the extent to which the views with regard to brand were considered.

Table 5.32: Age and the Extent to which Suggestions for any Brand were Considered

Age	Extent of Consideration of Suggestions for Brands		
	Somewhat Considered	Totally Considered	Total
< 18 years	11 (50.0)	11 (50.0)	22 (100.0)
19-25 years	32 (45.7)	38 (54.3)	70 (100.0)
26-35 years	43 (43.0)	57 (57.0)	100 (100.0)
36-50 years	33 (41.2)	47 (58.8)	80 (100.0)
> 50 years	11 (28.9)	27 (71.1)	38 (100.0)
Total	130 (41.9)	180 (58.1)	310 (100.0)

Note: Figures in parentheses represent the percentages

Education and the Extent to which Suggestions for any Brand were Considered

A cross tabulation with education of the influencers and the extent to which preference with regard to brand was considered in the final purchase is shown in Table 5.33.

When compared with the education levels of the influencer members, a reverse relationship is observed. As the education level of the members improves, a relatively smaller proportion feels that their views have been fully considered. This could be interpreted in the way that with higher education levels awareness also improves and each member's views on brands are formed after much research.

Any deviation in the brand selection due to family dynamics is likely to lead to a feeling that their views have not been fully considered. chi-square test shows that there is a significant difference between level of education and the extent to which preference with regard to brand was considered.

Table 5.33: Education and the Extent to which Suggestions for any Brand were Considered

Education	Extent of Consideration of Suggestions for Brands		
	Somewhat Considered	Totally Considered	Total
XII and below	31 (47.7)	34 (52.3)	65 (100.0)
Graduate	117 (64.6)	64 (35.4)	181 (100.0)
Post-Graduate	90 (67.7)	43 (32.3)	133 (100.0)
Professional	72 (80.9)	17 (19.1)	89 (100.0)
Total	310 (66.2)	158 (33.8)	468 (100.0)
chi-square = 18.9**			

** Significant at 0.01 level.
Note: Figures in parentheses represent the percentages

Sex and the Extent to which Suggestions for any Brand were Considered

A cross tabulation between sex of the influencers and the extent of consideration of views regarding brands in the final purchase is shown in Table 5.34.

It is clear from the table that there is not much difference in the male or female influencers with regard to the extent to which preference for brands was considered. chi-square test also does not show a significant difference between sex of the influencer and the extent to which preference for any brand was considered in the final purchase.

Table 5.34: Sex and the Extent to which Suggestions for any Brand were Considered

Sex	Extent of Consideration of Suggestions for Brands		
	Somewhat Considered	Totally Considered	Total
Male	79 (39.7)	120 (60.3)	199 (100.0)
Female	51 (45.9)	60 (54.1)	111 (100.0)
Total	130 (41.9)	180 (58.1)	310 (100.0)

Note: Figures in parentheses represent the percentages

Occupation and the Extent to which Suggestions for any Brand were Considered

A cross tabulation with occupation of the influencers and the extent of consideration of views regarding brands in the final purchase is shown in Table 5.35.

It is clear from the table that there is not much variation in the extent to which the views regarding the brands were considered in the final purchase and the influencers' occupation. chi-square test also did not find a significant difference.

Family Size and the Extent to which Suggestions for any Brand were Considered

A cross tabulation between the family size and the extent of consideration of views regarding brands in the final purchase is shown in Table 5.36.

It is clear from the table that as the family size changes there is not much difference in the extent to which their preference for brands has been considered. chi-square test does not show a significant difference between the influencers family size and the extent to which preference for a brand was considered.

Table 5.35: Occupation and the Extent to which Suggestions for any Brand were Considered

Occupation	Extent of Consideration of Suggestions for Brands		
	Somewhat Considered	Totally Considered	Total
Government Servant	21 (33.9)	41 (66.1)	62 (100.0)
Own Business	18 (46.1)	21 (53.9)	39 (100.0)
Self Employed Professional	10 (33.3)	20 (66.7)	30 (100.0)
Housewife	25 (52.1)	44 (64.7)	68 (100.0)
Student	32 (50.8)	23 (47.9)	48 (100.0)
Others#	24 (35.3)	31 (49.2)	63 (100.0)
Total	130 (41.9)	180 (58.1)	310 (100.0)

Note: Figures in parentheses represent the percentages
'Others' denotes influencers working in private concern and retired persons.

Product and the Extent to which Suggestions for any Brand were Considered

A cross tabulation with the product of the influencer and the extent to which preference for any brand was considered is shown in Table 5.37.

Table 5.36: Family Size and the Extent to which Suggestions for any Brand were Considered

Family Size	Extent of Consideration of Suggestions for Brands		
	Somewhat Considered	Totally Considered	Total
Two	14 (35.9)	25 (64.1)	39 (100.0)
Three	34 (49.3)	35 (50.7)	69 (100.0)
Four	41 (40.6)	60 (59.4)	101 (100.0)
Five	31 (47.0)	35 (53.0)	66 (100.0)
> Six	10 (28.6)	25 (71.4)	35 (100.0)
Total	130 (41.9)	180 (58.1)	310 (100.0)

Note: Figures in parentheses represent the percentages.

Table 5.37: Product and the Extent to which Suggestions for any Brand were Considered

Product	Extent of Consideration of Suggestions for Brands		
	Somewhat Considered	Totally Considered	Total
Audio System	17 (30.9)	38 (69.1)	55 (100.0)
Car	24 (46.2)	28 (53.8)	52 (100.0)
Personal Computer	24 (60.0)	16 (40.0)	40 (100.0)
Refrigerator	29 (49.1)	30 (50.9)	59 (100.0)
Television	15 (30.6)	34 (69.4)	49 (100.0)
Washing Machine	21 (38.2)	34 (61.8)	55 (100.0)
Total	130 (41.9)	180 (58.1)	310 (100.0)
chi-square = 12.6*			

*Significant at 0.05 level

It is clear from the table that in the case of television, audio system and washing machine the influencers have been found to be quite satisfied with the consideration of their views with regard to the brand as compared to other product categories. chi-square test also shows a significant difference with regard to various durable products and the influencers views with regard to the consideration of brand preference.

Sources of Information

Various sources used by the influencers to collect the necessary information regarding brands are shown in Table 5.38.

Table 5.38: Sources of Information (N=310)

Sources of Information	Frequency	Percent
Advertisements	207	66.8
Friends and Relatives	227	73.2
Past usage	48	15.5
Any other	40	12.9

Note: Multiple responses

The table depicts that most of the influencers used word of mouth (73.2 percent) i.e. feedback from friends and relatives as their source while collecting information regarding brands [1]. This is an important input for the marketers so that they should ensure that their customers feel satisfied long after the sale has taken place. An investment in after sales service always pays in the long run by keeping the customers satisfied. 207 (66.8 percent) influencer members have cited advertisements as source of information regarding brands. Experience from past usage and other (includes dealers, company sales persons and technical literature) have been cited by a relatively smaller number of respondents (at 12.9 percent and 15.5 percent respectively) as their sources of information regarding brands.

Suggestions for the Place of Purchase

Among various aspects regarding the purchase decision, store from where the product should be purchased is also important. The influencers were asked if they made any suggestions regarding the store from where the purchase should be made. Responses to this question are shown in the Table 5.39.

Table 5.39: Suggestions for the Place of Purchase

Suggestion Regarding the Store to Purchase from	Frequency	Percent
Yes	194	41.5
No	274	58.5
Total	468	100.0

Only 41.5 percent of the influencer members made any suggestions regarding the store from where the product should be purchased from. When compared with other two aspects where influencers have made their suggestions, viz. technical aspects of the product and the brands to be considered, much lesser influencers have given their views

about the store to purchase from. It can be interpreted that the selection of the point of purchase comes much later in the decision-making process.

Nature of Contribution of Influencers' Views – Solicited or Voluntary

All the 468 influencers were further asked whether their contribution was voluntary or if other members asked for their opinion. The response given by influencers is shown in Table 5.40.

Table 5.40: Nature of Contribution of Influencers' Views

Views	Frequency	Percent
Solicited	255	54.5
Voluntary	213	45.5
Total	468	100.0

The table reveals whether the contribution of views by the influencer members regarding the purchase was voluntary or solicited by other members. 255 (54.5 percent) influencers said that they were asked to collect the necessary information whereas 213 (45.5 percent) respondents said that they had collected the necessary information on their own and contributed voluntarily.

Further a cross tabulation was made between personal demographic characteristics and nature of influencers' views whether they were voluntary or solicited.

Income and Nature of Contribution of Influencers' Views

A cross tabulation was done between the monthly household income and the nature of the contribution of the influencers' views is shown in Table 5.41.

Table 5.41: Income and Nature of Contribution of Influencers' Views

Monthly Household Income (Rs.)	Nature of Contribution of Influencers' Views		
	Solicited	Voluntary	Total
< 10,000	24 (42.9)	32 (57.1)	56 (100.0)
10,001-15,000	58 (63.7)	33 (36.3)	91 (100.0)
15,001-20,000	75 (58.6)	53 (41.4)	128 (100.0)
20,001-25,000	38 (54.3)	32 (45.7)	70 (100.0)
> 25,000	60 (48.8)	63 (51.2)	123 (100.0)
Total	255 (54.5)	213 (45.5)	468 (100.0)

Note: Figures in parentheses represent the percentages

The table depicts that a larger proportion of the influencers in the monthly household income category of Rs. 10,001-15,000 had contributed their views when asked as compared to others where a higher proportion contributed their views voluntarily. chi-square test however does not show a significant difference between the monthly household income and the views related to purchase of the product.

Age and Nature of Contribution of Influencers' Views

A cross tabulation showing age of the influencer and nature of contribution of influencers' views is shown in Table 5.42.

Table 5.42: Age and Nature of Contribution of Influencers' Views

Age	Nature of Contribution of Influencers' Views		
	Solicited	Contributed Voluntarily	Total
< 18 years	16 (38.1)	26 (61.9)	42 (100.0)
19-25 years	60 (53.6)	52 (46.4)	112 (100.0)
26-35 years	70 (50.4)	69 (49.6)	139 (100.0)
36-50 years	62 (54.9)	51 (45.1)	113 (100.0)
> 50 years	47 (75.8)	15 (24.2)	62 (100.0)
Total	255 (54.5)	213 (45.5)	468 (100.0)
chi-square = 16.9**			

**Significant at 0.01 level.

Note: Figures in parentheses represent the percentages.

It is clear from the table that more of the influencers who are in the age group of eighteen or less than that have contributed their views voluntarily towards the purchase of product. For influencers in the age group of 19-50 years proportion contributing their views voluntary is similar to the overall average. When the influencers' age is more than 50 years there is more of solicited behaviour. chi-square test shows a significant difference with age of the influencers and the nature of their views related to purchase of product.

Education and Nature of Contribution of Influencers' Views

A cross tabulation showing the education of the influencers and nature of contribution of influencers' views is given in Table 5.43.

Table 5.43: Education and Nature of Contribution of Influencers' Views

Education	Nature of Contribution of Influencers' Views		
	Solicited	Voluntary	Total
XII and below	32 (49.2)	33 (50.8)	65 (100.0)
Graduate	109 (60.2)	72 (39.8)	181 (100.0)
Post-Graduate	76 (57.1)	57 (42.9)	133 (100.0)
Professional	38 (42.7)	51 (57.3)	89 (100.0)
Total	255 (54.5)	213 (45.5)	468 (100.0)
chi-square = 8.5*			

*Significant at 0.05 level
Note: Figures in parentheses represent the percentages

The table shows that when the influencer is a graduate his contribution is solicited in relatively more cases. In other cases when the influencer has studied up to class XII or below or when he is a post-graduate or when he is a professional there is no significant difference with education level with regard to the nature of his views related to purchase. chi-square test is significant at 0.05 level showing a significant difference with the education of the influencer and the nature of the views with regard to the purchase of the product.

Sex and Nature of Contribution of Influencers' Views

A cross tabulation showing the sex of the influencers and nature of contribution of influencers' views is shown in Table 5.44.

Table 5.44: Sex and Nature of Contribution of Influencers' Views

Sex	Nature of Contribution of Influencers' Views		
	Solicited	Contributed Voluntarily	Total
Male	127 (51.0)	122 (49.0)	249 (100.0)
Female	128 (58.4)	91 (41.6)	219 (100.0)
Total	255 (54.5)	213 (45.5)	468 (100.0)

Note: Figures in parentheses represent the percentages

It is clear from the table that there is not much difference in the male or female influencers' and nature of contribution related to the purchase of the product. chi-square test does not show a significant difference between sex of the influencer and the nature of views on the matter related to purchase of the product.

Occupation and Nature of Contribution of Influencers' Views

A cross tabulation with occupation of the influencers and nature of contribution of influencers' views is shown in Table 5.45.

Table 5.45: Occupation and Nature of Contribution of Influencers' Views

Occupation	Nature of Contribution of Influencers' Views		
	Solicited	Voluntary	Total
Government Servant	46 (54.1)	39 (45.9)	85 (100.0)
Own Business	32 (57.1)	24 (42.9)	56 (100.0)
Self Employed Professional	26 (65.0)	14 (35.0)	40 (100.0)
Working in Private Concern	32 (43.2)	42 (56.8)	74 (100.0)
Retired	7 (53.8)	6 (46.2)	13 (100.0)
Housewife	61 (65.6)	32 (34.4)	93 (100.0)
Student	51 (47.7)	56 (52.3)	107 (100.0)
Total	255 (54.5)	213 (45.5)	468 (100.0)
Chi-square = 12.4*			

*Significant at 0.05 level
Note: Figures in parentheses represent the percentages

It is clear from the table that when the influencer is a self employed professional or a housewife, there are more cases of solicited behaviour as compared to the cases of other occupations. chi-square test shows a significant difference on account of the influencers' occupation and nature of contribution of influencers' views regarding the purchase of the product.

Family Size and Nature of Contribution of Influencers' Views

A cross tabulation showing the family size of the and nature of contribution of influencers' views is shown in Table 5.46.

Table 5.46: Family Size and Nature of Contribution of Influencers' Views

Family Size	Nature of Contribution of Influencers' Views		
	Solicited	Voluntary	Total
Two	16 (30.2)	37 (69.8)	53 (100.0)
Three	59 (57.8)	43 (42.2)	102 (100.0)
Four	86 (53.1)	76 (46.9)	162 (100.0)
Five	54 (55.7)	43 (44.3)	97 (100.0)
>= Six	40 (74.1)	14 (25.9)	54 (100.0)
Total	255 (54.5)	213 (45.5)	468 (100.0)
chi-square = 21.6**			

**Significant at 0.01 level
Note: Figures in parentheses represent the percentages

It is clear from the table that with the change in the family size and nature of contribution of influencers' views with regard to the purchase also vary. When the family size is two, there is more voluntary behaviour regarding the purchase of product. When the size of the family is large, having six or more members, a larger proportion of the influencers contributed only when asked by other members. chi-square test shows a significant difference with regard to the family size and nature of contribution of influencers' views with regard to the purchase of product.

Product and Nature of Contribution of Influencers' Views

A cross tabulation showing the different product and nature of contribution of influencers' views on the matters related to purchase is shown in Table 5.47.

It can be seen from the table that a relatively larger proportion of the influencers made their contribution voluntarily when the products being considered by the family were cars and personal computers.

Although in all other products a larger proportion gave their views only when they were solicited, the proportion was relatively much higher in the case of washing machines and audio systems. chi-square test shows a significant difference with regard to the type of product when the nature of contribution of influencers' views with regard to the purchase of product is considered.

Family Members Soliciting Influencers' Views

Out of 468 influencers, 255 did not contribute voluntarily but were asked for their views related to brands or the technical aspects about the product (Table 5.40). It is common in a family purchase situation to involve different members in the decision-making process. At the same time certain members may be asked for their views for which they have to collect certain information. It is important to know which member actually seeks the views of other members. This person then acts as a coordinator who will ensure the involvement of various members so that there is post-purchase acceptance of the product by all members. The family members who asked these influencers for their views are shown in Table 5.48.

Table 5.47: Product and Nature of Contribution of Influencers' Views

Product	Nature of Contribution of Influencers' Views		
	Solicited	Voluntary	Total
Audio system	51 (63.0)	30 (37.0)	81 (100.00
Car	35 (45.5)	42 (54.5)	77 (100.0)
Personal Computer	23 (41.8)	32 (58.2)	55 (100.0)
Refrigerator	49 (55.1)	40 (44.9)	89 (100.0)
Television	37 (52.1)	34 (47.9)	71 (100.0)
Washing Machine	60 (63.2)	35 (36.8)	95 (100.0)
Total	255 (54.5)	213 (45.5)	468 (100.0)
Chi-square = 11.5*			

*Significant at 0.05 level
Note: Figures in parentheses represent the percentages

All the 255 (54.5 percent) influencers who said that the views on the matters related to purchase were solicited were further asked about which family members asked for their views. It turns out that it is the husband who takes on the role of the coordinator as mentioned above in 59.2 percent of the cases followed by the wife who does so in 47.5 cases.

Table 5.48: Family Members Soliciting Influencers' View (N=255)

Family	Frequency	Percent
Husband	151	59.2
Wife	121	47.5
Child 1	89	34.9
Child 2	44	17.25
Child 3	7	2.7
Grand	26	10.1
Member A	10	3.9

Note: Multiple Responses

Conclusion

As an influencer, a family member is expected to affect different aspects of the purchased product viz. the features to be considered, brands to be preferred and place to purchase the product from. Almost all types of members have acted as influencers with no fixed profile although there were more of younger members and students. Children turned out to be the main influencers in the case of personal computer, audio system and television whereas the wife contributed in all products except in the case of personal computer. A large number of influencers made contributions regarding the technical aspects of the product. More male members were found to give technical suggestions. Most influencers who contributed on the technical aspects covered parameters such as performance, features and quality. Around sixty percent of these influencers felt that their views on the technical aspects were completely considered while purchasing the product. Extent of consideration of the influencers suggestions regarding technical aspects seemed to depend upon their age and occupation and were found to be much higher in case of television as compared to other products.

A large number of influencer members also contributed their suggestions regarding the brands to be preferred. Influencers' contribution regarding the brand depended upon the demographic variables such as age, education, occupation and sex. Extent to which the influencers' brand preference was considered depended upon the family income and the education level of the member. Around sixty percent members felt that their views regarding brands were considered especially in case of colour television, audio system and washing machine. Word of mouth turned out to be the most important source of information, closely followed by advertisements in different media. Compared to the technical aspects and the brands, a lesser number of influencers made their suggestions regarding the place of purchase.

A large percentage of the influencers contributed their views only when they were solicited. Voluntary contribution of the views by the influencers depends upon the age, education, occupation and the family size. There was more voluntary contribution of views in case of car and personal computer by the influencer members. The person who emerged as the coordinator in the purchase process by seeking the views of other members is the husband. Members acting as influencers, corresponding to the stage of information search of the decision-making process are very important for the marketer. At this stage the family dynamics come into play and every member tries to get his own views considered in the final purchase. The marketer must ensure that he is able to evoke a positive response from different members for his brand.

Note

1. Harish Bijoor, "Inside Indian Marketing: Word of Mouth ", ***The Economic Times,*** January 22, 2001, p. 13.

6

Buying Roles: The Decider

As the family progresses with the decision-making process, on the basis of the information collected in the previous stages, a member assumes the responsibility of finally deciding the characteristics of the product to be purchased. This stage arrives after the purchase intentions are confirmed and a decision taken to satisfy one or more family members' need for the product.

The person who decides to execute the intentions will make up certain purchase sub-decisions viz., brand decision, vendor decision, timing decision and payment method decision. The person assuming the decider's role consults other members of the family to glean the information that they have collected either voluntarily or as per the instructions of other members. The aspects on which the family members are consulted also vary from member to member and the product under consideration.

Although various members of the family act as influencers offering their opinions and gathering information, it is finally the decider who sifts this information for his/her use. It shall be interesting to note which person takes on the role of the decider in an Indian family in the decision-making process for the purchase of consumer durable products.

The role of a decider corresponds to the stage IV (purchase decision) of the decision-making process:

Need Recognition →	Information Search →	Evaluation of Alternatives →	Purchase Decision →	Post-purchase Behaviour
Initiators				
	Influencers			
				Decider

The role of the decider is very important for the family, as the decision-maker is responsible for the trade-off with alternative products. In such a situation, the decider is the final authority on the product to be purchased.

Characteristics of the Decider

The demographic characteristics of various deciders are shown in Table 6.1. In total there are 321 deciders which have different characteristics.

Table 6.1:Characteristics of Deciders (Respondents)

Characteristics	**Frequency**	**Percent**
SEX		
Male	274	85.4
Female	47	14.6
AGE		
Less than 25 years	30	8.9
26-35 years	97	30.2
36-50 years	113	35.2
More than 50 years	81	25.3
Education		
<=Graduate	106	33.0
Post Graduate	119	37.1
Professional e.g.,	96	29.9
Occupation		
Government Service	107	33.3
Own Business	101	31.5
Working in Private	66	20.6
Others	47	14.6

From the table it can be deduced that the decider in an Indian family for the purchase of a consumer durable is typically a male member who is more than 25 years of age, reasonably educated and has his own business or is in the government service.

At this stage one may interpret that a typical Indian family is male dominated especially when it comes to finally decide about the purchase of an expensive household item such as a consumer durable product. Although more female members are now working, the main breadwinner in the Indian families is still a male member. For a high value product in the family, main financial contribution is likely to come from the male members, thus explaining their high proportion as the deciders in the study.

Another observation can be made that there are a few families where more than two members have acted as the decider (total 321 deciders in 313 families with at least one decider per family). This means that in most families the deciding authority rests with one member, who is male in most cases. 90.7 percent of the total decider members are over 25 years of age and 60.5 percent were aged over 35 years which means that a senior member in the family is more likely to act as the decider.

Member-wise Status of Deciders

Out of a total of 321 deciders the member-wise classification of deciders is shown in Table 6.2. The table reveals that out of a total of 321 deciders, majority are the husband 230 (71.7 percent), which is being followed by the wife in 41 (12.8 percent) cases. Children have acted as deciders in 36 (11.3 percent) cases.

Table 6.2: Member-wise Status of Deciders

Member	Frequency	Percent
Husband	230	71.7
Wife	41	12.8
Child 1	31	9.7
Child 2	5	1.6
Grand father	12	3.7
Member A	2	0.6
Total	321	100.0

This part of the decision-making process has the husband as undisputed protagonist. The husband turns out to be the final decider in the Indian families' decision-making process for consumer durable products in most cases.

Indian families are typically patriarchal. Other family members may participate in the decision-making process for purchasing a consumer durable product in the initial stages but when it comes to finally deciding on various aspects of the purchasing decision, it is the father who prevails.

The decision-making process is quite democratic in its initial stages where different members had expressed their desires for a new product or participated actively as influencers. However when it comes to making the final decision regarding different aspects of the purchase it is the husband who is responsible.

Decider Member vis-à-vis Product Purchased

A cross-tabulation was made between the decider member and the product purchased which is shown in Table 6.3. As can be seen from the table, in most of the products the husband has been the decider except in the case of television. In case of television a relatively larger number of other members (42 percent) have acted as deciders. Television in India is at a maturity stage of the PLC and has fairly high level of penetration. Most of the family members are familiar with the product and it is one of the main sources of entertainment in a family. It is hence quite likely that members other than the husband also act as deciders in the purchase of a television.

Table 6.3: Decider Member vis-à-vis Product Purchased

Product Purchased	**Decider**		
	Husband	Others#	Total
Audio System	41 (71.9)	16 (28.1)	57 (100.0)
Car	48 (88.9)	6 (11.1)	54 (100.0)
Personal Computer	32 (69.6)	14 (30.4)	46 (100.0)
Refrigerator	42 (71.2)	17 (23.7)	59 (100.0)
Television	29 (58.0)	21 (42.0)	50 (100.0)
Washing Machine	38 (69.1)	17 (30.9)	55 (100.0)
Total	230 (71.7)	91 (28.3)	321 (100.0)
chi-square = 12.8*			

*Significant at 0.05 level.
Note: Figures in parentheses represent the percentages.
#'Others' comprise of wife, children, grand parents and other members.

While purchasing a car in the family husband has been the decider in 88.9 percent cases, which is the highest among all the six products considered. One of the reasons for this could be that the car is the most expensive of all the items considered in the study. Secondly, as we shall see in the study later, the husband is the main user of the car in the family.

In case of refrigerators and washing machines where the wife is clearly the main user, it is still the husband who acts as the final decider in as high as 71.2 percent and 69.1 percent cases respectively. This could mean that the wife in the Indian families looks up to the husband to make the final decision once she has expressed her need and given all the details for the product.

In case of products audio system and personal computers, refrigerator, personal computer and washing machine the husband has played an active role. But in the case of television members other than the husband have acted as decision-makers in 42 percent cases. chi-square test also shows a significant difference between the various durable products and the family members who have acted as decision-makers.

Factors Considered While Purchasing The Product

The factors considered by the decider while purchasing the product are shown in Table 6.4. The deciders were asked to choose from various factors that were considered while finally deciding about the product to be purchased. When compared to a similar question (Table 5.12) asked to the influencers, it can be seen that the pattern of the responses is more or less repeated. Although performance has retained its position, with 80 percent deciders mentioning it, the positions of the features and quality have interchanged with substantially larger number of deciders preferring it as compared to the influencers (81.3 percent deciders considered quality while making the decision as compared to 72.6 percent influencers).

Table 6.4: Factors Considered while Purchasing the Product (N=321)

Factors Considered	Frequency	Percent
Features	239	74.5
Quality	261	81.3
Performance	267	83.2
Ease of operation	107	33.3
Aesthetics	83	25.9
After-sales Service	184	57.3
Price	268	83.5
Overall	12	3.7

Note: Multiple Responses

Price as a factor was introduced in the case of deciders and the highest number of the respondents (83.5 percent) considered it while making the decision. A substantially higher proportion of the deciders (57.3 percent) considered after sales service as compared to the influencers (40.9 percent, Table 5.12). Aesthetics and ease of operation were considered by a relatively smaller proportion of the deciders (25.9 percent and 33.3 percent, respectively).

Regarding the product characteristics considered by the decider members, we can say that his approach is much more balanced as compared to the influencers; price emerges as the most important factor, quality scores over the features and after sales service is given its due importance.

Trade-off Among Alternative Products

Deciders were asked to mention if they had made a trade-off with any other product while purchasing the current product. The views of deciders on this aspect are shown in Table 6.5.

Table 6.5: trade-off among Alternative\Products

Views with Regard to trade-off	Frequency	Percent
Yes	57	17.8
No	264	82.2
Total	321	100.0

It can be seen from the table that at this stage of the decision-making process a relatively much smaller proportion of deciders (17.8 percent) had to consider a trade-off with other products. It is interesting to compare this observation with the question put to the initiators asking them if their need for the product purchased was turned down in the past. In response to that 27.1 percent (Table 4.14) initiators mentioned that they had expressed their wish for the product in the past also when it was not considered. Thus, in 57 (17.8 percent) cases there was a conflict in the family related to the current purchase of the product.

Members Whose Views Were Considered by the Decider

Deciders were further asked about which family member's views they had considered on the following aspects. The views of family members, which were considered by the decider, are shown in Table 6.6.

Table 6.6 reveals the family members whom the decider chose to consult on different aspects while making the final purchase decision. The table is divided into three parts each corresponding to different deciding members viz., husband, wife and others which includes the children and grand parents. Different aspects of the products on which the opinion is sought include features, brand, model, price to be paid and place from where the purchase should be made.

Table 6.6: Views of which Family Members Considered (N = 321)

Family Members	**Factors Decider Member: Husband (230)**				
	Brand	Model	Features	Price to be paid	Where to buy
Wife	150 (65.2)	126 (54.8)	141 (61.3)	117 (50.9)	57 (24.8)
Child 1	119 (51.7)	104 (45.2)	116 (50.4)	23 (10.0)	54 (23.5)
Child 2	60 (26.1)	58 (25.2)	61 (26.5)	8 (3.5)	10 (4.3)
Grand Parents	15 (6.5)	11 (4.8)	17 (7.4)	18 (7.8)	11 (4.8)
Member A	17 (7.4)	13 (5.7)	17 (7.4)	7 (3.0)	11 (4.8)
Family Members	**Factors Decider Member: Wife (41)**				
	Brand	Model	Features	Price to be paid	Where to buy
Husband	25 (61.0)	24 (58.5)	21 (51.2)	35 (85.4)	32 (78.0)
Child 1	17 (41.5)	15 (36.6)	13 (31.7)	5 (12.2)	5 (12.2)
Child 2	11 (26.8)	5 (12.2)	9 (22.0)		2 (4.9)
Grand Parents	3 (7.3)	2 (4.9)	3 (7.3)	2 (4.9)	1 (2.4)
Member A	3 (7.3)	2 (4.9)	2 (4.9)	1 (2.4)	1 (2.4)
Family Members	**Factors Decider Member: Children etc.(50)**				
	Brand	Model	Features	Price to be paid	Where to buy
Wife	16 (32.0)	12 (24.0)	16 (32.0)	7 (14.0)	4 (8.0)
Husband	21 (42.0)	18 (36.0)	24 (48.0)	33 (66.0)	22 (44.0)

Note: Figures in parentheses represent the percentages

As we have seen, the husband turns out to be the decider member in most families. It can be seen that relatively higher proportion of husbands have consulted their wife and children regarding the brand (65.2 percent and 77.8 percent with wife and children respectively) and the features (61.3 percent and 76.9 percent with wife and children respectively) of the product to be purchased. A relatively lesser numbers consulted them regarding the model of the product to be purchased (54.8 percent and 61.4 percent with wife and children respectively). However when it comes to the price of the product there has been a very low level of consultation by the husband, especially with the children. In only 13.5 percent cases the husband has consulted the children. It can be interpreted from the above that as far as the general aspects of the product such as brand, model or features are concerned the husband adopts an egalitarian approach but when it comes to the financial decision he reserves the right with himself. It is typical of any family to see the children as the spenders whereas the parents are supposed to provide the funds. When the husband reserves the right to decide about the price, it is possible that the product which is finally purchased may not confirm to the specifications given by other members which could result in some amount of dissatisfaction among them. As far as the place to purchase is concerned there is again a very low level of consultation by the husband (24.8 percent and 27.8 percent with wife and children respectively).

When the wife is the decider a similar pattern of consultation as in the case of the husband is observed with the positions of husband and wife interchanged, except that a very large number of wives (85.4 percent) have consulted their husbands regarding the price of the product. The wife as the decider member also did not consult the children on the price of the product. Regarding the place of purchase the wife extensively consulted the husband (78.0 percent).

When other family members (all members excluding the husband and wife) are the deciders there is almost an equal amount of consultation with the husband and wife regarding the brand, model and the features of the product to be purchased. For the price of the product and the place of purchase the husband is consulted in most of the cases.

Extent of Consultation for the Product Purchased

In the previous part we had asked the deciders to specify which members they consulted when they were making the final decision about various aspects of the product. This is however not sufficient to judge if the deciders approach was truly egalitarian or there were shades of autocratic behaviour. It is then important to find out the extent of consultation by the deciders. The deciders were asked to rate the extent to which they consulted other family members while making a decision to purchase the product. This is shown in Table 6.7.

Table 6.7: Extent of Consultation for the Product Purchased

Degree of Consultation	Frequency	Percent
Consulted Extensively	97	30.2
Consulted not so Extensively	94	29.3
Consulted only Selectively	74	23.1
Did not consult at all	56	17.5
Total	321	100.0

It can be seen from the table, that the deciders varied in the extent of consultation with other members. Whereas 17.5

percent deciders did not consult at all, 23.1 percent consulted selectively. Only 30.2 percent deciders consulted the other family members extensively on various aspects of the purchase. 29.3 percent deciders consulted other members although not so extensively.

The degree of consultation in the purchase of a product is a very important factor in the decision-making process. It was felt to study it in more detail as to how this factor is related to other variables such as demographic profile of consumers and type of product under consideration.

Degree of Consultation vis-à-vis Income

A cross tabulation was done between the monthly household income of the decider and the extent to which he consulted other family members. This is shown in Table 6.8.

Table 6.8: Deciders' Degree of Consultation vis-à-vis Income

Monthly Household Income (Rs.)	Degree of Consultation				
	Did not consult at all	Consulted only Selectively	Consulted not so Extensively	Consulted Extensively	Total
Less than or equal to 10,000	6 (16.2)	8 (21.6)	8 (21.6)	15 (40.5)	37 (100.0)
10,001-15,000	5 (9.1)	10 (18.2)	17 (30.9)	23 (41.8)	55 (100.0)
15,001-20,000	22 (25.6)	21 (24.4)	25 (29.1)	18 (20.9)	86 (100.0)
20,001-25,000	10 (18.5)	13 (24.1)	17 (31.5)	14 (25.9)	54 (100.0)
More than 25,000	13 (14.6)	22 (24.7)	27 (30.3)	27 (30.3)	89 (100.0)
Total	13 (17.4)	74 (23.1)	94 (29.3)	97 (30.2)	321 (100.0)

Note: Figures in parentheses represent the percentages

It can be seen from the table that a relatively higher proportion of the deciders with a monthly household income of less than 15;000 consulted other family members extensively (40.5 percent) in the income group of less than Rs. 10,000 and 41.8 percent in Rs. 10,001-15,000. In the other income groups however the rating given by the deciders on the extent of consultation is similar to the overall rating. chi-square test does not show a significant difference between monthly household income and the extent of consultation with other members by the decider.

Degree of Consultation vis-à-vis Age

A cross tabulation was done between the deciders' age and the extent to which he consulted other members while purchasing the durable product which is shown in Table 6.9.

Table 6.9: Degree of Consultation vis-à-vis Age

Age	Degree of Consultation				
	Did not consult at all	Consulted only Selectively	Consulted not so Extensively	Consulted Extensively	Total
Less than 25 years	10 (33.3)	8 (26.7)	8 (26.7)	4 (13.3)	30 (100.0)
26-35 years	23 (23.7)	22 (22.7)	23 (23.7)	29 (29.9)	97 (100.0)
36-50 years	17 (15)	31 (27.4)	34 (30.1)	31 (27.4)	113 (100.0)
More than 50 years	6 (7.4)	13 (16.0)	29 (35.8)	33 (40.7)	81 (100.0)
Total	56 (17.4)	74 (23.1)	94 (29.3)	97 (30.2)	321 (100.0)
chi-square =22.81**					

** Significant at .01 level. Figures in parentheses represent the percentages

Table 6.9 reveals that as the age of the decision-maker increases they consult other members extensively for the purchase of a durable product. When the age of the decider was 25 years or less than that the highest rating was given to no consultation from other family members. But with the rise in the age of the decision-maker there has been an increase in the degree of consultation amongst other family members.

chi-square value, which is significant at 0.01, shows that age of the decision-maker and the extent of consultation he makes with other family members differ significantly.

Degree of consultation vis-à-vis Education

The extent of education of deciders is another factor, which may have an impact on the extent of their consultation with other family members. A cross tabulation between degree of consultation vis-à-vis education of the decision-maker is shown in Table 6.10.

Table 6.10: Degree of consultation vis-à-vis Education

Education	Degree of consultation				
	Did not consult at all	Consulted only Selectively	Consulted not so Extensively	Consulted Extensively	Total
Up to Graduate	14 (13.2)	21 (19.8)	27 (25.5)	44 (41.5)	106 (100.0)
Post Graduate	18 (15.1)	27 (22.7)	43 (36.1)	31 (26.1)	119 (100.0)
Professional e.g., MBBS, CA, etc.	24 (25.0)	26 (27.1)	24 (25.0)	22 (22.9)	96 (100.0)
Total	56 (17.4)	74 (23.1)	94 (29.3)	97 (30.2)	321 (100.0)
chi-square =15.65*					

Significant at .05 level.

Note: Figures in parentheses represent the percentages

Table 6.10 reveals that the deciders' education level has an impact on the extent to which they consult other family members in the purchase of a consumer durable product. Degree of consultation is relatively more in case of the deciders whose education level is either graduation or lower. In case of professionals a relatively lower proportion of the respondents consulted other family members actively. 25 percent of the deciders in this group did not consult other members at all whereas 27.1 percent did so only selectively. Thus, with the rise in the education of the decider he consults other family members to a relatively lower extent for the purchase of a durable product.

chi-square value, which is significant at 0.05 level, shows that education and the degree of consultation differ significantly.

Degree of Consultation vis-à-vis Sex

A cross tabulation between extent to which other family members were consulted vis-à-vis sex of the decider is shown in Table 6.11.

Table 6.11: Degree of consultation vis-à-vis Sex

Sex	Degree of Consultation				
	Did not consult at all	Consulted only Selectively	Consulted not so Extensively	Consulted Extensively	Total
Male	50 (18.2)	61 (22.3)	81 (29.6)	82 (29.9)	274 (100.0)
Female	6 (12.8)	13 (27.7)	13 (27.7)	15 (31.9)	47 (100.0)
Total	56 (17.4)	74 (23.1)	94 (29.3)	97 (30.2)	321 (100.0)

Note: Figures in parentheses represent the percentages

Table 6.11 reveals that there is no difference amongst male and female decider members with regard to the degree of consultation they had with other family members in the purchase of a consumer durable product. Around 30 percent of both male and female family members have been found to consult other family members extensively.

Degree of consultation vis-à-vis Occupation

It was decided to consider occupation of the decider to see if this factor had any impact on the extent of consultation with other members by the decider while purchasing a durable product. A cross tabulation between degree of consultation vis-à-vis occupation of the decider is shown in Table 6.12.

Table 6.12: Degree of consultation vis-à-vis Occupation

Occupation	Degree of consultation				
	Did not consult at all	Consulted only Selectively	Consulted not so Extensively	Consulted Extensively	Total
Government Service	21 (19.6)	18 (16.8)	30 (28.0)	38 (35.5)	107 (100.0)
Own Business	14 (13.9)	24 (23.8)	33 (32.7)	30 (29.7)	101 (100.0)
Working in Private Concern	7 (14.9)	23 (34.8)	17 (25.8)	12 (18.2)	66 (100.0)
Others*	7 (14.9)	9 (19.1)	14 (29.8)	17 (36.2)	47 (100.0)
Total	56 (17.4)	74 (23.1)	94 (29.3)	97 (30.2)	321 (100.0)

Figures in parentheses are the percentages,
*Others include retired persons, housewives and students.

Table 6.12 depicts that the deciders in all the occupations other than those working in private firms, tend to consult other members extensively. A relatively smaller proportion of the decider members who are working in private firms consults other members. The chi-square test however does not show any difference in the extent of consultation with other members when compared with the occupations of the decider members.

Degree of Consultation vis-à-vis Family Size

A cross tabulation between degree of consultation vis-à-vis family size of the decider is shown in Table 6.13.

Table 6.13: Degree of Consultation vis-à-vis Family Size

Family Size	Degree of consultation				
	Did not Consult at all	Consulted only Selectively	Consulted not so Extensively	Consulted Extensively	Total
Two	15 (34.9)	9 (20.9)	10 (23.3)	9 (20.9)	43 (100.0)
Three	15 (21.1)	16 (22.5)	20 (28.2)	20 (28.2)	71 (100.0)
Four	16 (14.4)	31 (27.9)	37 (33.3)	27 (24.3)	111 (100.0)
> = Five	10 (10.4)	18 (18.8)	27 (28.1)	41 (42.7)	96 (100.0)
Total	56 (17.4)	74 (23.1)	94 (29.3)	97 (30.2)	321 (100.0)
chi-square =22.15**					

** Significant at .01 level

Note: Figures in parentheses represent the percentages

Table 6.13 reveals that as the family size increases, the decider members tend to be more consultative. When the family consists of two members, only 20.9 percent decider members consulted the other member extensively whereas in case of families with five or more members, 42.7 percent of the deciders consulted other family members extensively. chi-square value, which is significant at .01 level, shows that the degree of consultation differ significantly with the family size.

Degree of Consultation vis-à-vis Age, Education and Family size

In order to find out the effect of these three factors, namely, age, education and family size to the 'amount of consultation' by family members before the purchase of the product, **multiple regression,** was used. Table 6.14 shows the results of the determinants of consultation by other family members for the purchase of products.

Table 6.14: Determinants of Consultation with other Family Members for the Purchase of Durable Products

Independent Variable	**Dependent Variable: Extent of Consultation**		
	Beta	Simple r	t -Value
Age	0.21**	0.23**	3.83
Education	-0.19**	-0.18**	3.57
Family Size	0.14**	0.21**	2.61
Multiple R = 0.34 **R Square = 0.11**			

** Significant at .01 level.

Table 6.14 depicts that these three independent variables (age, education and family size) have contributed significantly to the dependent variable (extent of consultation with other family members). The beta value of age in the table (Beta = .21) shows that as the age of the decision-makers increases they tend to consult other family members extensively for the purchase of a durable product. Secondly, as the education of the decision-maker increases there is a decrease in the rate of consultation of family members for the purchase of a durable product. Thirdly, as the family size of decision-makers increases they tend to consult other family members extensively for the purchase of a durable product. The value of R square shows that the three variables (age, education and family size) contribute significantly to the dependent variable up to the extent of 11 percent.

Degree of Consultation vis-à-vis Product purchased

Data was collected with regard to six types of product categories, namely, audio system, car, personal computer, refrigerator, television and washing machine. A cross tabulation was made between the extent of consultation by the decider member and different product categories which is shown in Table 6.15.

From the table it can be seen that for the purchase of television a relatively higher proportion of the decider members (46 percent) consulted other family members extensively. Television is a joint usage product and views of other members in the family are likely to be considered important by the decider members. In case of washing machine and audio system also there is a relatively higher degree of consultation by the decider. A smaller proportion of the deciders was found to consult other family members in the purchase of a personal computer.

Table 6.15: Extent of consultation vis-à-vis Product Categories

Product Purchased	Degree of consultation				
	Did not consult at all	Consulted only Selectively	Consulted not so Extensively	Consulted Extensively	Total
Audio-system	13 (22.8)	8 (14.0)	18 (31.6)	18 (31.6)	57 (100.0)
Car	10 (18.5)	15 (27.8)	19 (35.2)	10 (18.5)	54 (100.0)
Personal Computer	13 (28.3)	13 (28.3)	12 (26.1)	8 (17.4)	46 (100.0)
Refrigerator	11 (18.6)	16 (27.1)	18 (30.5)	14 (23.7)	59 (100.0)
Television	3 (6.0)	9 (18.0)	15 (30.0)	23 (46.0)	50 (100.0)
Washing Machine	6 (10.9)	13 (23.6)	12 (21.8)	24 (43.6)	55 (100.0)
Total	56 (17.4)	74 (23.1)	94 (29.3)	97 (30.2)	321 (100.0)
Chi-square =28.47**					

** Significant at 0.01 level
Note: Figures in parentheses represent the percentages

Chi-square value, which is significant at 0.01 level, shows that the extent of consultation with other members by the decider differs significantly with different product.

Financial Contribution For The Purchase Of Product

At this stage it was decided to find out which of the family members contributed financially in the purchase of the product. The financial contribution made by different family members for the purchase of the product is shown in Table 6.16.

Table 6.16: Financial Contribution for the Purchase (N=313)

Family Member who made Contribution	Frequency	Percent
Wife	77	24.6
Husband	283	90.4
Children	34	10.9
Grand parents	26	8.3
Member A	3	0.9

Note: Multiple responses

Table 6.16 reveals that the financial contributory in majority of cases is the husband (90.4 percent) followed by the wife in 80 (24.6 percent) cases. Children have contributed financially in 34 (10.9 percent) cases while grand parents contributed in 27 (8.3 percent) cases.

To have a better insight into this stage of the decision-making process, we shall see the combinations in which the family members have contributed towards the purchase. This is shown in the Table 6.17.

It can be seen from the table that of the various combinations (of financial contribution), husband was the sole contributor in maximum number of cases (60.7 percent). In 15.66 percent cases both wife and husband contributed financially. Maximum number of members who have contributed financially in any of the cases studied by us, is three where the children or the grandparents have combined with the husband and wife to pay for the product. This could mean that even if the family is large, number of members who are going to contribute financially is not going to be more than three. Even this percentage is very small at 2.88 percent.

Table 6.17: Combinations of the Family Members who Contributed Financially

Combinations of the family members who contributed financially in the purchase.*	Frequency	Percent
Husband only	190	60.7
Wife only	13	4.15
Children only	13	4.15
Wife and Husband	49	15.66
Wife and Children	3	0.96
Wife and Grandparents	1	0.32
Husband, Wife and Children	2	0.64
Husband, wife and grandparents	7	2.24
Husband and children	16	5.11
Husband and grandparents	18	5.75
Husband and any other member	1	0.32
Total	313	100.00

*Values for the combinations other than those mentioned below were zero.

It can also be seen that in 69 percent of the cases it is going to be a single member who is going to pay for the product. Cases where any two members contribute for the purchase are 28.12 percent of which in around half of the cases it is the combination of the husband and wife.

When we look at the cases where either husband or the wife has contributed, there are 95.85 such cases. We can hence deduce that in around 96 percent of the cases either the husband or wives are the contributory members in the purchase of a consumer durable product. However, the husband is going to remain as the most important financial contributory in the family situation.

Conclusion

The decider member finally collates the information collected in the previous stages and decides about the various aspects of the product to be purchased. He is responsible for the trade-off between the views of different members and also among alternative products. The decider members turns out to be a male, mostly the husband, more than 25 years of age and reasonably educated. In most cases there was only one person who assumed the responsibility of the decider. Members in the role of decider differ with the products under consideration. Decider members considered price as the most important factor, closely followed by the aspects like performance and the quality of the product. Around 18 percent of the deciders had to make a trade-off with another product at this stage. It turned out that the deciders preferred different members for their views while making decisions regarding different aspects of the product. Although it was fairly a democratic approach while taking views regarding brand, model and features, it was the husband who was consulted the most regarding the price of the product. Husband as the decider member consulted his wife for her views on this aspect.

The extent of consultation, which is also an indicator of the degree of incorporation of other members' views, varied with deciders' age, education and family size. It also varied with different product categories. In case of certain products such as, television, washing machine and audio system there was a consultation to a higher extent by the decider members.

The financial contributory in majority of cases was husband, followed by wife and children. In cases where more than one members contributed financially it was primarily the combination of the 'husband and wife' which paid for the product.

It is important for the marketer to understand as to which all family members does the decider consult while making decisions on various aspects of the consumer durable product to be purchased. Since husband is the decider in most cases, irrespective of the type of consumer durable product, the marketer must study husband as a subject to understand him better. Since price turned out to be the most important factor for the deciders, the marketers should come out with innovative financing options for their brands.

7

Buying Roles: The Actual Buyer

In the context of this study, the term 'buyer' refers to the family member(s) who are physically involved in the process of purchasing a product. The purchase of a consumer durable product is an important occasion. Traditionally, in North India, it is considered auspicious to purchase a consumer durable product on *Dhanteras*, the day preceding *Diwali*, the festival of lights. Prayers are performed in the night and the purchased product is accorded due importance. Similar sentiments also prevail in other parts of the country on different important festivals. In view of these market characteristics and consumer behaviour, it can be expected that the responsibility of purchasing the product would be bestowed on the most important person in the household.

Although this is a very advanced stage in the decision-making process when most things have been discussed and decided about, the buyer is still exposed to the influence of the retailer. It is important to assess as to what extent the buyer is aware about the different aspects of the product to be purchased and how far the retailer is able to influence the purchase decision. Both these aspects have far-reaching implications for the marketer when he balances the push and pull selling strategies.

The role of a buyer corresponds to the stage IV (purchase decision) of the decision-making process:

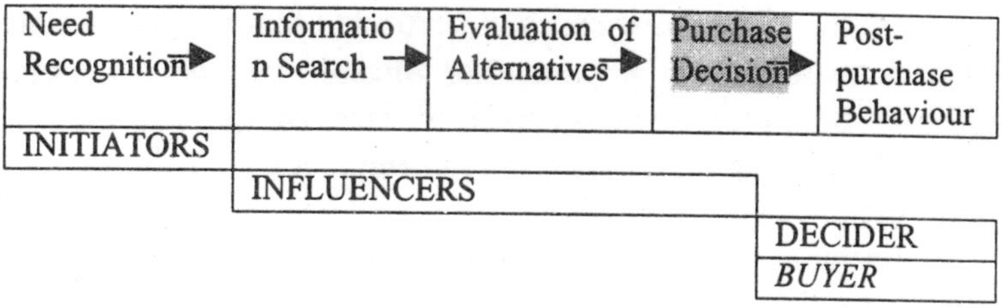

The product finally purchased by the buyer shall decide subsequent post-purchase behaviour.

Characteristics of the Buyer

Demographic characteristics of the buyer members are shown in Table 7.1.

Table 7.1: Characteristics of Buyers (Respondents)

Characteristics	Frequency	Percent
SEX		
Male	296	91.6
Female	27	8.4
AGE		
Less than 25 years	29	8.9
26-35 years	98	30.3
36-50 years	119	36.8
More than 50 years	77	23.8
EDUCATION		
>=Graduate	101	31.2
Post Graduate	116	35.9
Professional e.g., MBBS, CA, etc.	106	32.8
OCCUPATION		
Govt. Service	105	32.5
Own Business	111	34.4
Working in Pvt. Concern	71	22
Others	36	11.1

From the table 7.1 it can be interpreted that a buyer in the case of purchase of a consumer durable product is more likely to be a male member over 30 years of age, reasonably well educated and having a government job or running his own business.

As in the case of the decider, male members dominate the role of the buyer. A buyer's role involves activities outside home where one has to physically go to purchase the product. Traditionally, in the Indian families, all activities outside home fall in the domain of the male members, although it is changing fast. Maximum number of the buyer members fall in the age group of 36-50 years which could mean that this responsibility is taken up by a more mature and experienced family member. A buyer has to understand the requirements of different members about the product, select the place of purchase, negotiate with the dealer and purchase the product. As it can be seen that there are 323 buyers for 313 families where purchase took place. This implies that in ten families there were two buyers. On inquiring it was found that in ten families both the buyer members insisted that they had played equally active role in the process and they were not merely accompanying each other. This kind of a situation is possible when there are conflicting views of both the members. Ferber observed similar situation in one of his studies [1].

Member-wise Status Of Buyers

Out of a total of 323 buyers, the member-wise classification is shown in Table 7.2.

As can be seen from the above table, buyer's role in a family for the purchase of a consumer durable product is dominated by the husband (76.5 percent). When compared with the role of the decider (Table 6.2), a similar member-wise constitution can be seen in the buyer's role. The husband's role has become even more prominent (from 71.7 percent in decider to 76.5 percent in buyer) while the wife role has reduced even further prominent (from 12.8 percent in decider to 6.8 percent in buyer). Number of children participating in this role has also gone up marginally from 9.7 percent to 12.1 percent.

Table 7.2: Member-wise Status of Buyers

Member	Frequency	Percent
Husband	247	76.5
Wife	22	6.8
Child 1	33	10.2
Child 2	6	1.9
Grand father	8	2.5
Grand mother	1	0.3
Member A	6	1.9
Total	323	100.0

Buyer Member vis-à-vis the Product Purchased

It was decided to find out if the members in the buyer's role change with different products or the same pattern is applicable universally for all consumer durable products.

A cross tabulation between the buyer member vis-à-vis the product purchased was done which is shown in Table 7.3. Since the buyer's role has been predominantly played by the husband, for statistical reasons it was decided to divide the family members in two parts viz. husband and others (which includes wife, children, grandparents and other relations).

Table 7.3: Buyer Member vis-à-vis Product Purchased

Purchased Product	Buyers		
	Husband	Others#	Total
Audio-system	39 (69.6)	17 (30.4)	56 (100.0)
Car	51 (94.4)	3 (5.5)	54 (100.0)
Personal Computer	33 (73.3)	12 (26.7)	45 (100.0)
Refrigerator	48 (81.4)	11 (18.6)	59 (100.0)
Television	32 (58.2)	23 (41.8)	55 (100.0)
Washing Machine	44 (81.5)	10 (18.5)	54 (100.0)
Total	247 (76.5)	76 (23.5)	323 (100.0)
Chi-square =23.15**			

**Significant at .01 level
Note: Figures in parentheses represent the percentages
#'Others' comprise of wife, children, grand parents and other members.

Although husband is undoubtedly more prominent in the buyer's role, a relatively higher proportion of the other members have been the buyers in case of audio system (30.4 percent), personal computer (26.7 percent) and television (41.8 percent). In case of car it seems to be an all husband affair with other members contributing a mere 5.5 percent in the buyer's role. It is interesting to note that in both the wife-dominated products viz. refrigerator and washing machine, a relatively higher proportion of the husbands have acted as the buyers. chi-square test shows a significant difference in the member playing buyer's role with different products.

Buyer's Product-Rating

It is important to note how much is the buyer member clear about different aspects of the purchase when he sets out to purchase the product. Buyers were asked to rate on a five-point scale about the clarity on different aspects when they went to purchase the product. The buyers' rating on the aspects is shown in Table 7.4.

Table 7.4: Buyer's Product-Rating (N = 323)

Buyer's Rating	Features	Brand	Price Range	Where to buy from
Absolutely Clear 5	197 (61.0)	232 (71.8)	190 (58.8)	163 (50.5)
4	89 (27.6)	65 (20.1)	80 (24.8)	76 (23.5)
3	32 (9.9)	18 (5.6)	38 (11.8)	48 (14.9)
2	2 (.6)	4 (1.2)	3 (0.9)	15 (4.6)
1 Not clear at all	3 (.9)	4 (1.2)	12 (3.7)	21 (6.5)

Note: Figures in parentheses represent the percentages

It can be seen from the table that a reasonably large proportion of the buyers have a clarity about the features of the product and the brand to be purchased. The buyers were also moderately clear about the price to be paid for the product but a relatively smaller proportion of the buyers was clear about the place to purchase the product from.

For a marketer who has to decide between the pull and push strategy for his consumer durable brand it is important to note that 71.8 percent of the buyers are absolutely clear about the brand to be purchased. Another 20.1 percent also have a reasonable clarity about the brand, leaving only 8.1 percent of the buyers to be influenced by the dealer at the point of purchase.

Regarding the features of the product and the price to be paid it seems that there is a reasonable clarity to a large number of buyers. It is likely that they have a shortlist of the features they want in their product and have a price range within which they expect the product to fall.

Number of buyers who are clear about the place of purchase are relatively lesser when compared to other factors. This could reflect on the loyalty towards the dealers and retail counters. There are several factors which can be considered while selecting the outlet for the purchase of a consumer durable product. Some of the important factors are proximity, past experience, prominence of the showroom, display of products, brands dealing in and behaviour of the dealer and the sales person.

Family Members Accompanying The Buyer

Purchase of a consumer durable product is a special occasion in a family. A lot of excitement is expected and it is likely that other family members may accompany the buyer to actually purchase the product. Table 7.5 shows which family members accompanied the buyer.

Table 7.5 depicts various combinations of the family members who had gone to actually purchase the consumer durable product for the family. It can be seen from the table that there are 17 such independent combinations of family members. Out of the 313 cases of purchase, in 58.5 percent cases two members, in 23.32 percent cases only one member, in 15.02 cases three members and in 1.9 percent cases four members had gone for the purchase.

Table 7.5: Member Groups who went for the Purchase (N = 313)

Members who went for the purchase	Frequency	Percent
Buyer Member: Husband N = 247		
Alone	38	15.38
With Wife only****	98	39.68
With Children only****	56	22.67
With Grandparents only*	4	1.62
With 'Other members' only	6	2.43
Together With Wife and Children	35	14.17
Together with Wife and Grandparents	4	1.62
Together with Wife and 'Other Member'	1	0.40
Together with Wife and Children and 'Other Member'	1	0.40
Together with Wife and Children and Grandparents	4	1.62
Buyer Member: Wife N = 22		
Alone	4	18.18
With Husband only	9	40.91
With Children*	5	22.73
With Husband and Children	3	13.64
With Husband and Grandparents	1	4.55

Buyer Member: Children N = 39		
Alone	29	74.36
With Husband	7	17.95
With Wife	3	7.69
Buyer Member: Grandfather/Grandmother N = 9		
With 'Husband'	1	11.11
With 'Wife'	1	11.11
With Children	4	44.44
With 'Husband' and 'Wife'	2	22.22
With 'Husband' and 'Wife' and 'Children'	1	11.11
Buyer Member: 'Other Members' N = 6		
Alone	2	33.33
With Husband	1	16.67
With Children	2	33.33
With Husband and Wife	1	16.67

Note: Number of stars (*) in the table represent the repetition of the groups where both the members claimed to be the buyers. There are ten such cases. Therefore total number of different groups after correcting for above-mentioned duplicity is 313, same as total number of families.

It is significant that out of 73 single member cases, in 29 cases (39.7 percent) there were children. Also, when seen in the context where the children were buyers, in 75 percent cases they went to purchase the product alone. This shows that a large proportion of the children preferred to shop alone.

When we look at the most preferred companion, we find that the wife has accompanied one or the other member in 45.6 percent cases while the children have gone along with others in 35.5 percent cases. When wife was the buyer she had husband as companion in 59.1 percent cases where as only 17.95 children as buyers preferred to take the father along.

We can also see that wife and husband as buyers found each other as the most preferred partners whereas the children went alone to purchase the product. When we relate the buyer members with different products (Table 7.3) the above mentioned finding has important implications for the marketer and the retailer as well. They can decide their services and selling strategies accordingly for different products.

Dealer's Opinion At The Time Of Purchase

At the time of purchase the buyer is exposed to the influence of the dealer at the retail outlet that can change his decision about the product. It should be understood that the dealer is likely to have his own interests while selling his merchandise. Margins available to a dealer vary with the brands depending upon the incentives given by the manufacturers. This further depends upon the sale that the dealer is able to make of a particular brand. It is obvious then that the dealer may try to change the decision of the buyer into buying a brand or a model in which he makes higher margins. It should also be noted that the dealer is also an expert about the consumer durable products and the buyer is likely to consult the dealer on certain aspects. Table 7.6 shows the frequency of the buyers who consulted the dealer at the time of purchase.

Table 7.6: Dealer's Opinion at the Time of Purchase

Opinion of the Dealer	Frequency	Percent
Yes	202	62.5
No	121	37.5
Total	323	100.0

It can be seen from the table that a large proportion of the buyers consulted the dealer (62.5 percent) for his opinion regarding the product to be purchased. When we consider the clarity of the buyers on various aspects (Table 7.4), we see that some percentage of the buyers is not totally clear about certain aspects when they set out to purchase the product. These buyers are likely to consult the dealer before they finally make up their mind.

Effect of the Discussion with the Dealer

Buyers were asked if their decision about the product purchased changed after discussion with the dealer. Table 7.7 shows the views of the buyers with regard to the discussion with the dealer.

Table 7.7: Discussion with the Dealer (N=202)

Decision Change	Frequency	Percent
Yes	42	21.0
No	160	79.0

We can see from the table that 79 percent of the buyers did not change their decision about the product after discussion with the dealer. However 21 percent did change their decision to some extent (brand or model) after taking dealer's opinion. This is an important feedback for the marketers that the dealers can not be totally ruled out if they can sway the decision of 21 percent of the buyers. Hence it is also important for the marketers to ensure that they have satisfied channel partners.

Conclusion

Buying of a consumer durable product is an important occasion and in several Indian families it is considered auspicious to purchase one during important festivals like Diwali. Buyer is a person who is physically involved in the process of going to the retail counter and purchasing the product. He is expected to be clear about different aspects of the product and has to select one that shall meet the expectations of several members in the family. He is also exposed to the influence of the retailer with whom he has to negotiate the price of the product, most suitable for the family.

The member in the role of a buyer is more likely to be a male, mostly husband, over 30 years of age and reasonably well educated. There can be more than one person acting as buyers in a family in case of a conflicting situation, but such instances are only a few. Whether it is the husband or any other family member in the buyers' role depends, upon the type of the product to be purchased. Whereas husband is predominantly the buyer in case of a car, refrigerator and washing machine, a large number of other members act as buyers in case of audio system, personal computer and television.

Most of the buyers were clear about the features and the brand of the product to be purchased. Relatively smaller proportions of the buyers were clear about the place to purchase the product from. In most of the cases the buyer was accompanied by one more member, however the number of persons who went for the purchase was as high as four. Husband and wife as buyers found each other as the most preferred partner when they went for the purchase. A large percent of children as buyers preferred to shop alone. Although a large number of buyers took the opinion of the dealer most of them did not change their decision. This is an important feedback for the marketer who has to decide between the push and pull strategy. Although the dealer cannot change the opinion of most of the buyers, a satisfied channel partner can go a long way in strengthening a brands' perception in the mind of the consumer.

Note

1. Robert Ferber, "On the Reliability of Responses Secured in Sample Surveys", ***Journal of the American Statistical Association***, September 1955, pp.788-810.

8

Buying Roles: The Product User

In the context of the purchase of a consumer durable product in a family, the user is the person who uses the purchased product. Although almost all the members of a family are beneficiaries of the product, it is imperative to identify who actually qualifies as the end-user of the product. All the persons in the family may be benefited by a washing machine but all do not qualify to be its user. A user is a person, who has a thorough operational knowledge of the product, can control its performance and can maintain the product to ensure its efficient functioning.

In case of the purchase of a consumer durable product in a family, it is important to know how satisfied the user is with different aspects of the product. Since so many members have influenced the purchase decision, it is possible that user satisfaction may vary on different counts. For instance, children may be the real users of an audio system that has been purchased after the collective influence of various family members. The children may or may not be fully satisfied with the product, which is reflected in their post-purchase behaviour.

The users may or may not recommend the product to others on the basis of their satisfaction levels. This has serious implications for the marketer since word of mouth plays a very important role in the purchase of consumer durable products.

The role of a user corresponds to the stage V (Post-purchase behaviour) of the decision-making process:

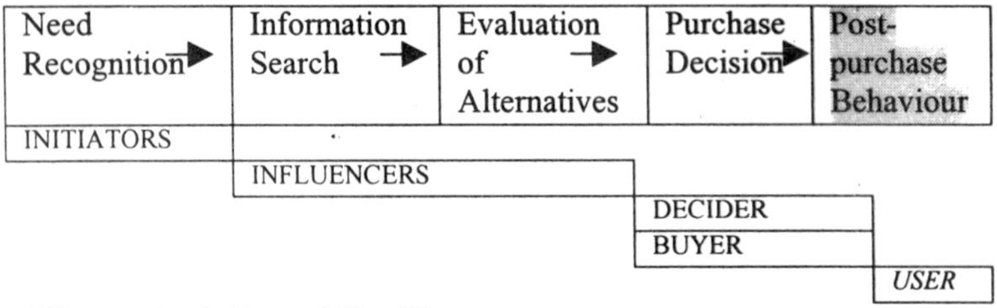

Characteristics of the User

The demographic characteristics of various users are summarised in Table 8.1.

Table 8.1: Characteristics of Users (Respondents)

Characteristics	Frequency	Percent
SEX		
Male	359	46.7
Female	409	53.3
AGE		
Less than 18 years	142	18.5
19-25 years	181	23.6
26-35 years	174	22.7
36-50 years	160	20.8
More than 50 years	111	14.5
EDUCATION		
< XII	210	27.3
Graduate	271	35.3
Post Graduate	171	22.3
Professional e.g., MBBS, CA, etc.	116	15.1
OCCUPATION		
Govt. Service	127	16.5
Own Business	69	9.0
Self Employed Professional	49	6.4
Working in Private Concern	95	12.4
Retired	17	2.2
Housewife	160	20.8
Student	251	32.7

Table 8.1 shows the characteristics of the user members. We can see from the above that there is a fairly uniform distribution of the user members across the variables sex and age. When considering educational level, a relatively higher proportion of the user members are either graduates (35.3 percent) or have studied (or studying) below XII standard (27.3 percent) while only 15.1 percent are the professionals. By occupation, a very large proportion of the user members is either students (32.7 percent) or housewives (20.8 percent).

It can be noticed that there is no clear profile of the user member and that anybody in the household can be a user for the consumer durable product. In the following matter we shall see if there is any variation for different types of the products.

Member-wise Status of Users

Out of a total of 768 users, the member-wise status is shown in the Table 8.2.

Table 8.2: Member-wise Status of Users

Member	Frequency	Percent
Husband	163	21.2
Wife	216	28.1
Child 1	179	23.3
Child 2	108	14.1
Child 3	29	3.8
Grand father	20	2.6
Grand mother	21	2.7
Member A	25	3.3
Member B	7	0.9
Total	768	100.0

Table 8.2 reveals that out of a total of 768 user members, maximum number are children in 316 (41.1 percent) cases followed by the wife in 216 (28.1 percent) cases and the husband in 163 (21.2 percent) cases. It is important to note that the children are the active users in maximum number of cases for the durable products at home. It means that they assume several responsibilities attached with the product after the purchase. Wife is also an active user member that is expected since traditionally the wife in Indian families is responsible for various products at home. Grand parents have acted as users in 41 (5.3 percent) cases and other family members have acted as user in only 32 (4.2 percent).

User Member vis-à-vis the Product Purchased

A cross tabulation was done amongst the user member vis-à-vis the six product categories to find out which family members are actually the users for the product. This is shown in Table 8.3.

Table 8.3 reveals that different family members are the active users for different products. It can be seen that in case of audio system and personal computer children (55.1 percent and 62.5 percent respectively) dominate as users. Husband turned out to be the main user in case of the car (53.9 percent) while the wife emerged as the dominant user in case of washing machine. In case of the television, compared to other products, there is relatively a uniform distribution of the members as users. Maximum number of the users in case of refrigerator turned out to be children (37.5 percent) closely followed by the wives (33.5 percent). We can see that there is relatively a uniform participation by different members in case of television and refrigerator while there is usually one member who dominates as user in case of rest of the products. This observation can help us classify these products as wife-dominated, husband-dominated, children-dominated and common-usage consumer durable products.

Table 8.3: User Member vis-à-vis the Durable Product

Product Purchased	User Member				
	Husband	Wife	Children	Others#	Total
Audio System	21 (15.2)	35 (25.4)	76 (55.1)	6 (4.3)	138 (100.0)
Car	48 (53.9)	18 (20.2)	17 (19.1)	6 (6.7)	89 (100.0)
Personal Computer	20 (20.8)	11 (11.5)	60 (62.5)	5 (5.2)	96 (100.0)
Refrigerator	28 (15.9)	59 (33.5)	66 (37.5)	23 (13.1)	176 (100.0)
Television	39 (22.3)	44 (25.1)	64 (36.6)	28 (16.0)	175 (100.0)
Washing Machine	7 (7.4)	49 (52.1)	30 (31.9)	8 (8.5)	94 (100.0)
Total	163 (21.2)	216 (28.1)	313 (40.8)	76 (9.9)	768 (100.0)
chi-square = 146.28**					

** Significant at 0.01 level.
Note: Figures in parentheses represent the percentages
#'Others' comprise of grand parents and other members.

Chi-square test shows a significant difference in the product and the members who act as its users, at 0.01 level.

Users' Satisfaction on Product Aspects

Users were asked to specify their level of satisfaction on a 3-point scale with regard to six different aspects of the consumer durable product purchased in the family. The users' post-purchase satisfaction from the durable product is shown in Table 8.4.

Table 8.4: Users' Satisfaction on Product Aspects

Users Rating	Quality	Features	Perfor-mance	Ease of operation	Ease of mainte-nance	Aesth-etics
High	571 (74.3)	563 (73.3)	566 (73.7)	502 (65.4)	470 (61.2)	535 (69.7)
Medium	169 (22.0)	148 (19.3)	167 (21.7)	212 (27.7)	226 (29.4)	174 (22.7)
Low	28 (3.6)	57 (7.4)	35 (4.6)	54 (6.9)	72 (9.4)	59 (7.7)

Note: Figures in parentheses represent the percentages

It can be seen from the above table that there is a uniform pattern of the proportion of the users at different satisfaction levels on some aspects viz. quality, features, performance and aesthetics. A high proportion of the users (around 70 percent) mentioned that had a high level of satisfaction on these aspects. As far as other aspects viz. ease of operation and ease of maintenance are concerned there is a relatively smaller proportion of the users who experienced a high level of satisfaction (65.4 percent and 61.2 percent respectively). Earlier, both the influencer members and the decider members were asked to specify the aspects they considered while making suggestions or while making the decisions. Ease of operation was one of them. It should be noted that in both the cases this aspect was not considered by a relatively large proportion of the influencer and the decider members. This could then be the reason for a relatively lower level of satisfaction of the user members on this aspect.

Users' Post-Purchase Satisfaction

In addition to the feedback on the satisfaction level derived from the aspects mentioned above the user members were also asked to specify their overall level of satisfaction from the product purchased. It was decided to ask this question in order to capture the impact of factors not covered in the previous section. A three-point scale was used and the response is shown in Table 8.5.

We can see from the above Table that there is a marked difference between the overall satisfaction derived from the purchased product and the level of satisfaction obtained from different aspects of the product, taken individually. Although the proportion of user members at the middle level remains the same at around 20 percent there is a steep fall in the number of user members with very high level of satisfaction and a corresponding rise in the number of users who experienced low levels of satisfaction.

Table 8.5: Users' Post-Purchase Satisfaction

Users Satisfaction	Frequency	Per cent
High	414	53.9
Medium	200	26.0
Low	154	20.1
Total	768	100.0

Recommendation for the Product to Others

Users were asked if they would recommend the purchased product to their friends and relatives. The views of the users whether they would like to recommend the purchased product to their friends and relatives or not are shown in Table 8.6.

Table 8.6: Recommendation for the Product to Others (N=768)

Recommendation	Frequency	Percent
Yes	747	97.3
No	21	2.7

Table 8.6 depicts that only a small number of users of the six durable products said that they would not recommend the product to their friends and relatives. 97.3 percent of the users said they would recommend the product to their friends and relatives.

Conclusion

User is a member who is not just a beneficiary of the product but who also has its thorough operational knowledge, can control its performance and also maintains it. There is a fairly uniform distribution of the users among different family members across the demographic variables such as, sex and age. The user members however vary with different products. Whereas the children are dominant users in case of audio system and personal computer, the husband and wife were found to be the main users of the car and washing machine respectively. In case of television there is a relatively uniform distribution of the members as users. Users had rated a reasonably higher level of satisfaction on quality, features and performance of the product purchased as compared to ease of operation and maintenance. For different products users satisfaction level also varies quite significantly on various aspects. Whereas washing machine and television were rated relatively higher on the performance aspects, personal computers scored much lower on satisfaction on this aspect. Factors like ease of operation and maintenance which received lesser consideration earlier from the influencer and decider members, were rated relatively lower on satisfaction by the users. Overall post-purchase satisfaction of the users depends upon the monthly household income and their educational level. Level of overall satisfaction also varies with the type of product purchased. Most of the members felt that they would recommend the product purchased to their friends and relatives despite the fact that around twenty percent of the users had mentioned a low level of overall satisfaction obtained from the product.

User members are important for the marketer as the satisfaction level of this group governs a positive or negative word of mouth. The marketers must ensure post-purchase satisfaction of the users by interacting with them on regular basis and in different forums. Several microwave manufacturers provide cookery classes to their users. BPL makes its microwave users a member of the 'wavelength club' which provides them with vital information regarding latest developments, tips about using the product in a better manner and new recipes.

9

Implications for Marketing Strategies

This chapter intends to present the summary and conclusions of the study. The roles which family members play in the purchase of a consumer durable product and implications of the findings for the marketer are given in the following paragraphs.

For a marketer chasing a winning promotion, it is important to understand the influence of family members on product purchase decisions. In India, where joint and nuclear families exist together, the marketer seeking to seize the future needs to focus not just on the individual but people defined by their positions, relationships and roles in the context of their families. Therefore, the real customer for the marketer is not the man or the woman or the child but the family as a whole.

Summary of Buying Roles

In the study, five roles (as defined by Kotler, namely, initiator, influencer, decider, buyer and user) played by family members in the purchase of a durable product are examined. In the purchase of a durable product, many family members are actively involved in the decision-making process at different stages. Indian families are quite different from the western families in the sense that empty nest stage of the family life cycle is not very common. On the contrary, large numbers of Indian families have three generations staying together. Family bonds are found to be very strong in our society. Decision-making process for the purchase of a consumer durable product is quite elaborate, as there are more members whose views need to be taken. It was found that the roles played by different members of the family varied with demographic parameters as well as with the types of products. This variation is observed both within a role and across the roles. Some members are found to be more active in certain roles. Major findings of the study pertaining to different roles are as follows:

Initiator

The initiator member is the one who starts the process in the family which ultimately leads to the purchase of the consumer durable product. The initiator is typically a young female member who is likely to be either the housewife or one of the children in the family. Need for audio system, personal computer and television is likely to be first expressed by the children in the family whereas the wife is more likely to initiate the process for the purchase of a refrigerator and washing machine. Husband has turned out to be the initiating member for the purchase of car.

Initiators first mentioned the need to purchase the product to the husband in majority of cases. It can be construed that most members see the husband to play an important role later in the decision-making process. At the same time it belies the assumption that the head of the family is not easily accessible. On the contrary, he seems to be most easily approachable in this context and the initiator considered it important to share its need about the product with him.

The time taken to culminate the purchase of the durable product after the initiator mentioned the need depends on demographic profile of both the initiators and the family as a whole. Average time taken in the purchase of a consumer durable product in a family is around six weeks that further depends on the monthly household income and the price of the product. Further, the time taken to purchase also depends upon the age of the initiating member and the type of product purchased. Factors such as sex and education of the initiators and family size do not have a significant impact the time taken to purchase the product.

It is found that the time taken to purchase car and personal computer is two months or more whereas the time taken to purchase television and washing machine is much less at one month or less.

Among the various reasons cited by the initiators to purchase a durable product, convenience and replacement of the existing product (because of the availability of new product with advanced features) emerged as most important. Around one in four initiators had expressed the need for the same product in the past also when it was not considered in the family. The purchase was postponed primarily because of insufficient funds. Another reason for postponement was that the family felt that the need for the product was not so strong at that point of time.

A large number of initiators mentioned the products' need in terms of type, features and functions however, only sixty percent felt that their needs were fully met from the purchased product. It is found that the time taken to purchase the product was higher in case of the initiators who remarked that they were somewhat satisfied with the purchased product as compared to those who felt that they were fully satisfied. This signifies that specifications of the product given by the initiator are likely to change during the decision-making process due to family dynamics involving requirements of other members and financial constraints.

Influencer

As an influencer a family member is expected to affect different aspects of the purchased product viz. the features to be considered, brands to be preferred and place to purchase the product from. Almost all types of members have acted as influencers with no fixed profile although there were more of younger members and students. Children turned out to be the main influencers in the case of personal computer, audio system and television whereas the wife contributed in all products except in the case of personal computer. A large number of influencers made contributions regarding the technical aspects of the product. More male members were found to give technical suggestions. Most influencers who contributed on the technical aspects covered parameters such as performance, features and quality. Around sixty percent of these influencers felt that their views on the technical aspects were completely considered while purchasing the product. Extent of consideration of the influencers suggestions regarding technical aspects seemed to depend upon their age and occupation and were found to be much higher in case of television as compared to other products.

A large number of influencer members also contributed their suggestions regarding the brands to be preferred. Influencers' contribution regarding the brand depended upon the demographic variables such as age, education, occupation and sex. Extent to which the influencers' brand preference was considered depended upon the family income and the education level of the member. Around sixty percent members felt that their views regarding brands were considered especially in case of colour television, audio system and washing machine. Word of mouth turned out to be the most important source of information, closely followed by advertisements in different media. Compared to the technical aspects and the brands, a lesser number of influencers made their suggestions regarding the place of purchase.

A large percentage of the influencers contributed their views only when they were solicited. Voluntary contribution of the views by the influencers depends upon the age, education, occupation and the family size. Age played an important role in determining whether the influencer member presents his/her views voluntarily or whether they are solicited. Younger members of the family contribute voluntarily whereas views of the elderly were solicited.

Among different products, in case of audio system and washing machines, lesser number of influencers contributed their views voluntarily. Voluntary contribution by the influencer members is higher in the case of smaller families. The person who emerged as the coordinator in the purchase process by seeking the views of other members is the husband. Members acting as influencers, corresponding to the stage of information search of the decision-making process are very important for the marketer. At this stage the family dynamics come into play and every member tries to get his own views considered in the final purchase. The marketer must ensure that he is able to evoke a positive response from different members for his brand.

Decider

The decider member finally collates the information collected in the previous stages and decides about the various aspects of the product to be purchased. He is responsible for the trade-off between the views of different members and also among alternative products. The decider members turns out to be a male, mostly the husband, more than 25 years of age and reasonably educated. In most cases there was only one person who assumed the responsibility of the decider. Members in the role of decider differ with the products under consideration. Decider members considered price as the most important factor, closely followed by the aspects like performance and the quality of the product. Around 18 percent of the deciders had to make a trade-off with another product at this stage. It turned out that the deciders preferred different members for their views while making decisions regarding different aspects of the product. Although it was fairly a democratic approach while taking views regarding brand, model and features, it was the husband who was consulted the most regarding the price of the product. Husband as the decider member consulted his wife for her views on this aspect.

It is found that the decision to purchase a consumer durable involves a lot of consultation amongst family members. The extent of consultation, which is also an indicator of the degree of consideration of other members' views, varied with deciders' age, education and family size. By the use of multiple regression it was found out that age, education and family size contribute significantly to the degree of consultation. It is found that higher the age of the decision-makers, more extensively does he consult other family members. Secondly, there is an inverse relationship of the extent of consultation with the education level of the decision-maker. Thirdly, as the family size increases, degree of consultation also increases.

The extent of consultation differs amongst the product categories. Television being a joint usage product has the highest rate of consultation, followed by washing machine. In case of the personal computer the degree of consultation amongst family members is found to be low.

The financial contributory in majority of cases was husband, followed by wife and children. With earning members increasing in the families the financial contribution for the product comes from a joint pool with various members participating. In cases where more than one members' contributed financially it was primarily the combination of the 'husband and wife' that paid for the product.

It is important for the marketer to understand as to which family members does the decider consult while making decisions on various aspects of the consumer durable product to be purchased. Since husband is the decider in most cases, irrespective of the type of consumer durable product, the marketer must study husband as a subject to understand him better. Since price turned out to be the most important factor for the deciders, the marketers should come out with innovative financing options for their brands.

Buyer

Buying of a consumer durable product is an important occasion and in several Indian families it is considered auspicious to purchase one during important festivals like Diwali. Buyer is a person who is physically involved in the process of going to the retail counter and purchasing the product. He is expected to be clear about different aspects of the product and has to select one that shall meet the expectations of several members in the family. He is also exposed to the influence of the retailer with whom he has to negotiate the price of the product, most suitable for the family.

The member in the role of a buyer is more likely to be a male, mostly husband, over 30 years of age and reasonably well educated. There can be more than one person acting as buyers in a family in case of a conflicting situation, but such instances are only a few. Whether it is the husband or any other family member in the buyers' role depends, upon the type of the product to be purchased. Whereas husband is predominantly the buyer in case of a car, refrigerator and washing machine, a large number of other members act as buyers in case of audio system, personal computer and television.

Most of the buyers were clear about the features and the brand of the product to be purchased. Relatively smaller proportions of the buyers were clear about the place to purchase the product from. In most of the cases the buyer was accompanied by one more member, however the number of persons who went for the purchase was as high as four. Husband and wife as buyers found each other as the most preferred partner when they went for the purchase. A large percent of children as buyers preferred to shop alone. Although a large number of buyers took the opinion of the dealer most of them did not change their decision. This is an important feedback for the marketer who has to decide between the push and pull strategy. Although the dealer cannot change the opinion of most of the buyers, a satisfied channel partner can go a long way in strengthening a brands' perception in the mind of the consumer.

User

User is a member who is not just a beneficiary of the product but who also has its thorough operational knowledge, can control its performance and also maintains it. There is a fairly uniform distribution of the users among different family members across the demographic variables such as, sex and age. The user members however vary with different products. Whereas the children are dominant users in case of audio system and personal computer, the husband and wife have been found to be the main users of the car and washing machine respectively. In case of television there is a relatively uniform distribution of the members as users.

Users rated a reasonably higher level of satisfaction on quality, features and performance of the product purchased as compared to ease of operation and maintenance. For different products users satisfaction level also varies quite significantly on various aspects. Whereas washing machine and television were rated relatively higher on the performance aspects, personal computers scored much lower on satisfaction on this aspect. Factors like ease of operation and maintenance which received lesser consideration earlier from the influencer and decider members, have been rated relatively lower on satisfaction by the users. Overall post-purchase satisfaction of the users depends upon the monthly household income and their educational level. Level of overall satisfaction also varies with the type of product purchased. Most of the members felt that they would recommend the product purchased to their friends and relatives despite the fact that around twenty percent of the users had mentioned a low level of overall satisfaction obtained from the product.

User members are important for the marketer as the satisfaction level of this group governs a positive or negative word of mouth. The marketers must ensure post-purchase satisfaction of the users by interacting with them on regular basis and in different forums.

Various Implications for the Marketer

The findings of the study have various implications for the marketer. The knowledge of family buying roles is often very important for developing appropriate marketing strategies. The major findings of the study and their implications for various marketing strategies are discussed below.

Product-Member Relationships

It was found that some members play a more active role during certain stages of the buying process pertaining to different products. Once the need for a consumer durable product is identified and the process for purchase initiated by the members, postponement of the purchase takes place in about twenty-seven percent of the cases. The marketer can, thus, identify the members who play the role of an initiator for his product. He can then develop an appropriate communication strategy targeted at these members to evoke the desired response. The initiators for the purchase of items like an audio system, personal computer and television are mostly children. They were also found to be the main influencers and users in case of such products. Although the husband is the initiator for the purchase of a car, the wife acts as a major influencer. In the case of a car, television and personal computer, a major proportion of the influencers make voluntary contributions as compared to that for other products. The time taken for initiating the purchase decision in the case of certain products has also been found to be relatively lesser than that for other products. The least amount of time was taken in the purchase of a television and washing machine and the maximum for the purchase of a car and personal computer. Marketers can thus develop a suitable contact programme on the basis of the average time taken in the purchase of a particular product. During these contact programmes, certain selected members of the family can be offered answers to some frequently asked questions as also demonstrations of the product that they propose to buy.

It was also found during the course of the study that the purchase of certain products like a television or a washing machine entailed extensive consultation among different family members. The most popular source of information for the influencer members was found to be word of mouth, followed by advertisements. Marketers should therefore ensure that they make customers for life so that the latter not only buy their different products from time to time but also express their satisfaction with these products to others. Suitable post-purchase activities should thus be organised by the marketers to build long-term relationships with their customers. These activities can take the form of, say, free service camps by manufacturers of cars and air conditioners, cookery classes for customers of microwave ovens or software support offered by personal computer manufacturers.

Intra-Family Dynamics in the Purchase of a Consumer Durable Product

Indian families are usually large in size and are characterised by strong bonds between their members. It was seen during the study that while the purchase decision-making process is relatively democratic in the initial stages, it seems to subsequently become much more unilateral in terms of the role played by the decider. Within a family, for instance, the husband was found to be playing the highly significant roles of the coordinator, decider and the buyer. The husband acts as the coordinator in the decision-making process with both the initiators and influencers confiding their needs in him, resulting in his domination in the role of a decider. He also contributes financially in most cases.

A large proportion of the influencer members contributed their views only when the latter were solicited. It has been seen that more influencer members contribute voluntarily in a small family whereas the degree of consultation that the decider undertakes with other family members is usually higher in the case of large families which consist of more than five members. As the decider, the husband consulted other members to obtain their views on aspects like performance and features of the product concerned, but preferred to consult the wife regarding the price to be paid. Usually two members are expected to go for the purchase of a consumer durable product but children, as buyers, prefer to shop alone. It is important for the marketer to understand the intra-family dynamics and relationships at play in the purchase of a consumer durable product in order to be able to decide the appropriate marketing mix.

Impact of Demographic Variables

The study indicated the existence of a significant relationship between certain variables and different demographic factors. Members displaying certain demographic characteristics were found to be more dominant in certain roles or situations. The initiators for the purchase of consumer durable products are mostly women. Lower middle income families (with monthly household incomes of below Rs 10,000) take the least time to purchase a consumer durable product, after the initiating member has expressed the need for the purchase.

More of the male members are likely to make technical suggestions. The extent of consideration of the influencers' views increases with age. Most of the influencers, especially in the age group of 26-50 years, have individual opinions about the brands which must be considered before the actual purchase of a consumer durable product. Higher education among the prospective buyers leads to better brand consciousness. It has been observed that a greater number of male members are likely to be brand-conscious. Deciders in the higher age group tend to consult other members of the family regarding the product to be purchased, much more than their peers in the lower age segment. Depending upon the target segment for his product, the marketer can devise his marketing strategies on the basis of the behaviour of various family members in relation to different demographic variables.

Motives for the Purchase of a Product

While trying to identify the actual customer, it is also very important to find out what motivates the latter to purchase the product. It was found in the study that the main reason for the purchase of a durable product is convenience and the need to replace the existing product with a new product that incorporates more advanced features. Interestingly, where the replacement of existing products was concerned, most customers did not wait for the earlier product to become non-functional. It can thus be deduced that it is up to the marketers to introduce better products with technologically advanced features to facilitate the preponement of purchase decisions taken by several families. A trade-off with other competing products is seen in one out of five families at the time of purchase. A marketer is therefore not only competing with other brands in his product category but with altogether different product categories. The reasons for postponing the purchase of a consumer durable product by a family (in around twenty seven percent of the cases) include the non-availability of sufficient funds as also the fact that the initiator or one or more of the other family members did not feel a strong need for buying the product. The marketer can overcome these constraints by offering the reluctant customer attractive financing options and technologically superior products to motivate him to take the purchase decision.

Role of the Dealer

While deciding the marketing mix, a marketer also has to allocate funds for the push and pull initiatives. Push initiatives are aimed at the intermediary who is offered incentives to invest and sell selective products. It has, however, been found in the study that the role of the dealer in the decision-making process and his influence in the final purchase is quite limited. Usually, Sixty percent of the buyers consult dealers, but only twenty percent of them change their minds about the brand name or any other aspect of the product. This implies that instead of trade promotions, the marketer should lay an emphasis on effective advertising. A satisfied trade partner, however, would only help to strengthen the brand.

Post-Purchase Satisfaction

Since word of mouth was found to be the most popular source of information, assessing the post-purchase satisfaction of the customers assumes greater importance for the marketer. A relatively small number of users in proportion to the actual number of users are found to be fully satisfied with the ease of operation and maintenance of the product. A relatively small proportion of personal computer users was found to be satisfied with the performance of the product(s) that they had bought while a large number of personal computer users had a low satisfaction level with the manner in which the maintenance of the machine was carried out. It was seen that 40 percent of the influencers felt that their views on product design and usage were only partially considered by the manufacturers, while around forty percent of the initiators were found to be only somewhat satisfied with the product they had purchased.

Entire families as consumers also display certain homogenous characteristics irrespective of who their members are. All the purchase decisions, be they for buying products for personal consumption or for common use, ranging from which brand to be purchased in what quantities, how often, and from where it is to be purchased, entail the enactment of different roles played by various family members. Each precise role to be played varies according to the dynamics of a particular family, its lifestyle, the personalities of and the relationships between individual members, as also the nature of the product bought. The marketer must thus take the family into consideration while framing his marketing strategies.

Bibliography

Bibliography

Books

Assael, Henry, *Consumer Behaviour and Marketing Action*, 5th ed. (Kent Publishing Company, Boston, 1995).

Aggarwala, N. K., *Role of Family in Consumer Purchase Decisions*, Unpublished M. Phil. Dissertation, Delhi University, Department of Commerce,1978.

Bennett, Peter D., and Harold H. Kassarjian, *Consumer Behaviour* 8th ed. (Prentice-Hall of India, New Delhi, 1998).

Blood, Robert O., and Donald M. Wolfe, *Husbands and Wives: The Dynamics of Married Living* (The Free Press, Ill., USA, 1960).

Boyd, Harper W., *et al.*, *Marketing Research: Text and Cases*, 4th ed. (Richard D. Irwin, Homewood, Ill., 1990).

Churchill, Gilbert A., *Marketing Research: Methodological Foundations*,
5th ed. (The Dryden Press, New York, 1991).

Converse, Paul D., and Harvey W Huegy, *The Elements of Marketing*, 3rd ed. (Prentice-Hall, Englewood Cliffs, N.J., 1972).

Engel, James, F., and Roger D. Blackwell, *Consumer Behaviour*, 4th ed. (The Dryden Press, New York, 1982).

Freund, Rudolf J., and William J. Wilson, *Statistical Methods* (Academic Press, USA, 1997).

Green, Paul E., *et al.*, *Research for Marketing Decisions*, 5th ed. (Prentice-Hall of India, New Delhi, 1995).

Gupta, Keshav, *Dimensions of Marital Roles in Purchase Decisions*, Unpublished M. Phil. Dissertation, Delhi University, Department of Commerce, 1979.

Gupta, S. C., and V. K. Kapoor, *Fundamentals of Mathematical Statistics* (Sultan Chand and Sons, New Delhi, 1994).

Harrell, Gilbert, *Consumer Behaviour* (Harcourt Brace, New York, 1986).

Hawkins, Del I., *et al*, *Consumer Behaviour: Implications for Marketing Strategy*, 3rd ed. (Business Publications, Texas, USA, 1986).

Horton, Raymond L., *Buyer Behaviour: A Decision-Making Approach* (Charles E Merrill Publishing Company, New York, 1984).

Kashyap, Madhu, *Buying Behaviour of College Students: An Analysis of Youth Market*, Unpublished M. Phil. Dissertation, Delhi University, Department of Commerce, 1985.

Komarovsky, Mirra, *Consumer Behaviour:Household Decision-Making*, (Nelson N. Foot, University Press, New York, 1961).

Kothari, C. R., *Research Methodology: Methods and Techniques*, 2nd ed. (Wishwa Prakashan, New Delhi, 1995).

Kotler, Philip, *Marketing Management: Analysis, Planning, Implementation and Control*, 10th ed. (Prentice-Hall of India, New Delhi, 2000).

Levin, Richard I., and David S. Rubin, *Statistics for Management*, 5th ed. (Prentice-Hall of India, New Delhi, 1992).

Martin, Zober, *Marketing Management* (John Wiley and Sons, New York, 1964).

Mowen, John C., *Consumer Behaviour*, 3rd ed. (Macmillan Publishing Company, New York, 1993).

Nandhi, Mani Arul, *Purchasing Patterns of Adolescent Consumers*, Unpublished M. Phil. Dissertation, Delhi University, Department of Commerce, 1983.

Nic, N., N., *et al.*, *SPSS: Statistical Package for the Social Sciences* (McGraw-Hill Book Co., New York, 1975).

Paul, Peter J. and Olson C Jerry, *Consumer Behaviour: Marketing Strategy Perspectives* (Richard D. Irwin, Homewood, Ill., 1987).

Poonam, *Children Influence in Consumer Buying Behaviour*, Unpublished M. Phil. Dissertation, Delhi University, Department of Commerce, 1991.

Reynolds, Fred D., and William D. Wells, *Consumer Behaviour* (McGraw-Hill Book Company, 1977).

Robertson, Thomas S., and Harold H. Kassarjian, *Handbook of Consumer Behaviour* (Prentice-Hall, Englewood Cliffs, 1991).

Sheldon, Bernert Eleanor, *Family Economic Behaviour: Problems and Prospects* (J. B. Lippincott Co., Toronto 1972).

Schiffman, Leon G., and Leslie Lazar Kanuk, *Consumer Behaviour*, 6th ed. (Prentice-Hall of India, New Delhi, 1997).

Snedecor, George W., and William G. Cochran, *Statistical Methods*, 6th ed. (Iowa State University Press, Iowa, 1967).

Tull, Donald S., and Del I. Hawkins, *Marketing Research: Measurement and Method*, 3rd ed. (Macmillan, New York, 1984).

Wilkie, William L., *Consumer Behaviour*, 3rd ed. (John Wiley and Sons, New York, 1994).

Yadava, S. Surendar and K. N. S. Yadava, *Statistical Analysis for Social Sciences*, 2nd ed. (Manak Publications, Delhi, 1995).

Zaltman, Gerald, and Melanie Wallendorf, *Consumer Behaviour: Basic Findings and Management Implications* (John Wiley & Sons, New York, 1979).

Zeisel, Hans, *Say It with Figures*, 5th ed. (Harper and Row, New York, 1968).

Articles

Banerjee, Lopa, "Living Life on Hold", *The Economic Times: 'Brand Equity'*, February 27, 1998, p.3.

Beatty, Sharon E., and Salil Talpade, "Adolescent Influence in Family Decision-Making: A Replication with Extension", *Journal of Consumer Research*, Vol. 21 (September 1994), pp. 332-341.

Berey, Lewis A., and Richard W Pollay, " The Influencing Role of Child in Family Decision-Making", *Journal of Marketing Research*, Vol. 5 (February 1968), pp. 70-72.

Bhandari, Bhupesh, "Videocon's Big Battle", *Business World,* August 16, 1999, pp. 30-32.

Bijapurkar, Rama, "Youth Un-Niched", *The Economic Times: 'Brand Equity'*, April 6, 1999, p.3.

Bijoor, Harish, "Inside Indian Marketing: Word of Mouth", *The Economic Times,* January 22, 2001, p. 13.

Boyd, Rollins C., and Stephen J. Bahr, "A Theory of Power Relationships in Marriage", *Journal of Marriage and the Family*, November 1976, pp. 619-627.

BPL Ltd., *Annual Report 1998-99*, pp. 40-41.

Burns, Alvin, and Donald Granbois, " Factors Moderating the Resolution of Preference Conflict in Family Automobile Purchasing", *Journal of Marketing Research,* February 1977, pp. 68-77.

Burr, Pat L, and Burr, Richard M, "Parental Responses to Child Marketing", *Journal of Advertising Research,* Vol. 17 (December 1977), pp. 17-20.

"Car Sales Cross Six Lakh Mark in 1999-2000", *Business India,* May 1-14, 2000, p. 30.

Carrie, Goerne, "Marketers Try to Get More Creative in Reaching Teens", *Marketing News,* August 5, 1991, p.2.

Carron, Andre, and Scott Ward, "Gift Decisions by Kids and Parents", *Journal of Advertising Research*, Vol. 15 (August 1975), pp. 15-20.

Chakraborty, Aloknanda, "Springing Right Back: A Cover Report on Godrej GE", *Advertising and Marketing,* February 15, 1999, pp. 40-46.

Chopra, Pritika, "Luck Lustre: A Cover Report on LG Electronics", *Advertising and Marketing*, March 31, 1999, pp. 42-47.

Corfman, Kim P., "Perceptions of Relative Influence: Formation and Measurement", *Journal of Marketing Research*, Vol. 28 (May 1991), pp. 125-136.

Corfman, Kim P., and Donald R. Lehmann, "Models of Cooperative Group Decision-Making and Relative Influence: An Experimental Investigation of Family Purchase Decisions", *Journal of Consumer Research*, Vol. 14 (June 1987), pp. 1-13.

Cunningham, Isabella C. M. and Robert T Green, "Purchasing Roles in the U.S. Family: 1955 and 1973", *Journal of Marketing, Vol.* 38 (October 1974), pp. 61-64.

Curry, David J. and Michael B. Menasco, "Some Effects of Differing Information Processing Strategies on Husband-Wife Joint Decisions, *Journal of Consumer Research,* Vol. 6 (September 1979), pp. 192-203.

Davis, Harry L, "Dimensions of Marital Roles in Consumer Decision Making", *Journal of Marketing Research*, Vol. 7 (May 1970), pp.168-177.

Davis, Harry L. and Benny P. Rigaux, "Perception of Marital Roles in Decision Processes", *Journal of Consumer Research*, Vol. 1 (June 1974), pp. 51-62.

Davis, Harry L., *et al*, "An Anchoring and Adjustment Model of Spousal Predictions", *Journal of Consumer Research,* Vol.13 (June 1986), pp. 25-37.

Dhawan, Polomy, "Clues to Change: IRS 1995", *Advertising and Marketing*, Vol. 15 (March 1996), pp. 24-31.

Dhawan, Radhika, "Driving Partner", *Business World,* February 5, 2001, pp. 32-33.

Dobhal, Shailesh, "Selling to the New Urban Family", *Business Today,* February 22, 1999, pp. 66-81.

Ferber, Robert and Lucy Chao Lee, "Husband-Wife Influence in Family Purchasing Behaviour", *Journal of Consumer Research*, June 1974, pp.43-50.

Ferber, Robert, "On the Reliability of Responses Secured in Sample Surveys", *Journal of the American_Statistical Association*, Vol. 50 (September 1955), pp. 788-810.

Ferber, Robert, "Research on Household Behaviour", *American Economic Review*, Vol. 52 (March 1962), pp. 19-63.

Filiatrault, Pierre and J. R. Brent Ritchie, "Joint Purchasing Decisions: A Comparison of Influence Structure in Family and Couple Decision-Making Units", *Journal of Consumer Research,* Vol. 7 (September 1980), pp. 131-140.

Foxman, Ellen R., Patriya S. Tansuhaj and Karin M. Ekstrom, "Family Member's Perceptions of Adolescents Influence in Family Decision-Making", *Journal of Consumer Research*, Vol. 14 (March 1989), pp. 482- 491.

Ghosh, Indranil, "Net Gain", *Business India,* May 29-June 11, 2000, pp. 81-82.

Ghosh, Indranil, "Car Sales Cross Six Lakh Mark in 1999-2000", *Business India,* May 1-14, 2000, p. 30.

Ghosh, Indranil, "Uphill Tasks", *Business India,* July 24 - August 6, 2000, pp. 78-80.

"Family During Transition", http.lycos.com.

Green, Robert T., and Isabella C. M. Cunningham, " Feminine Role Perception and Family Purchasing Decisions", *Journal of Marketing Research*, Vol. 12 (August 1975), pp. 325-332.

Gupta, Nabankur, "The Buying Emotion", *The Economic Times: 'Brand Equity'*, December 16, 1998, p.1.

Hempel, Donald J., " Family Buying Decisions: A Cross-cultural Perspective", *Journal of Marketing Research,* Vol. 11 (August 1974), pp. 295-302.

Jayashankar, Mitu, "Audio Products: A Survey", *Advertising and Marketing,* November 1-15, 1997, pp. 54-58.

Jetley, Neerja, "Child is the Father of Marketing", *Outlook,* March 1, 1999,
pp. 78-82.

Kildegaard, Ingrid C., "A Household is Not a Family", *Journal of Advertising Research*, Vol. 7 (June 1967), pp. 44-46.

Kumar, Krishna, "Industry Analysis: Desktops and Notebooks", *Dataquest,* July 15, 2000, pp. 140-154.

Mahanta, Vinod, "Consumer Electronics: The Colour Fades", *Business Today,* December 6, 2000, p. 24.

"Maruti Stays Ahead of the Car Race", *The Hindustan Times,* June 3, 2000, p. 16.

Menasco, Michael B. and David J. Curry, "Utility and Choice: An Empirical study of Wife/Husband Decision-Making", *Journal of Consumer Research*, Vol. 16 (June 1989), pp. 87-96.

McCann, Pulse, "Future Tense", *The Economic Times: 'Brand Equity'*, January 11, 2000, p. 3.

Moschis, George P., "The Role of Family Communication in Consumer Socialisation of Children and Adolescents", *Journal of Consumer Research,* Vol. 11 (March 1985), pp. 898-913.

Mudgil, Varun, "Survey on Personal Computers: Preparing for Change", *Advertising and Marketing*, June 15, 1998, pp. 42-52.

Mukherjee, Arindam, "Selling Bits and PCs", *Advertising and Marketing* March 31, 1999, p. 41.

Narula, Manoj, "Whirl of a Time", *Business India,* May 15-28, 2000, pp. 88-90.

Nelson, Margaret C., "The Resolution of Conflict in Joint Purchase Decisions by Husbands And Wives: A Review and Empirical Test", *Advances in Consumer Research*, Vol. 15 (1988), pp. 436-441 in William L. Wilkie, "Household Influences", *Consumer Behaviour,* 3rd ed. (Wiley International Edition, New York, 1994), p. 404.

Nickelodeon, "Separate Research Studies Indicate Today's Kids Having Unprecedented Influence On Family Purchasing Decisions", *http://www.businesswire.com/webbox/bw.020899/1098564.htm*, December 1999, pp. 1-3.

Pande, Bhanu, "Spreading Wider: A Cover Report on Videocon", *Advertising and Marketing*, July 31, 1998, pp. 48-53.

Park, Whan C., "Joint Decisions in Home Purchasing: A Muddling-Through Process", *Journal of Consumer Research*, Vol. 9 (September 1982), pp. 151-162.

Park, Whan C., "A Conflict Resolution Choice Model", *Journal of Consumer Research*, Vol. 5 (September 1978), pp. 124-135.

Patrick, Murphy P., and Staples A. William, "A Modernised Family-Life-Cycle", *Journal of Consumer Research,* Vol. 6 (June 1979), pp. 12-22.

Paxton, Jennifer Gregan, and John Deborah Roedder, "Are Young Children Adaptive Decision-Makers: A Study of Age Differences in Information Search Behaviour", *Journal of Consumer Research*, Vol.21 (March 1995), pp. 567-579.

Povaiah, Roshun, "Fresh Focus: A Cover Report on BPL", *Advertising and Marketing,* September 30, 1999, pp. 35-41.

Poviah, Roshun, "People and Products: Homing In", *Advertising and Marketing,* May 31,1999, p. 14.

Qualls, William J., "Household Decision Behaviour: The Impact of Husbands and Wives Sex Role Orientation", *Journal of Consumer Research*, Vol. 14 (September 1987), pp. 264-279.

Rawla, Bharati, "What Makes Her Tick", *The Economic Times: 'Brand Equity'*, October 8-14, 1997, p. 3.

Raman, Rakeh, "Addressal Systems: Trends PC", *Advertising and Marketing*, February 16-28, 1997, pp. 56-57.

Raman, Rakesh, "Prosperity Patterns", *Advertising and Marketing*, February 1-15,1997, pp. 38-43.

Raman, Rakesh, "Computers for Free: Trends Personal Computers", *Advertising and Marketing,* December 31, 1996, pp. 106-107.

Rodrigues, Malika, "Kids Play", *The Economic Times: 'Brand Equity'*, August 23-29, 2000, p.3.

Seymour, Daniel, and Greg Lessne, "Spousal Conflict Arousal: Scale Development", *Journal of Consumer Research*, Vol. 11 (December 1984), pp. 810-821.

Sharp, H., and P. Mott, "Consumer Decisions in the Metropolitan Family", *Journal of Marketing*, Vol. 21 (October 1956), pp. 149-156.

Shuptrine, F.K., and G. Samuelson, "Dimensions of Marital Roles in Consumer Decision- Making: Revisited", *Journal of Marketing Research*, Vol. 13 (February 1976), pp. 87-91.

Sharma, Sanjeev, "Cars Are More Affordable Today", *The Economic* Times, May 29, 2000, p. 8.

Shatrujeet, N., "Counting on Consolidation: Electolux Strategy", *Advertising and Marketing,* May 15, 1999, pp. 54-57.

Singh, Kanwaldeep, "Auto Sales to Move in Slow Gear", *Sunday Times of India,* June 4, 2000, p. 16.

Sinha, Suveen, K., "Maruti in a Midnight Alley", *Business Today,* February 6, 2001, pp. 46-48.

Spiro, Rosann L., "Persuasion in Family Decision-Making", *Journal of Consumer Research*, March 1983, pp. 393-402.

Sprey, Jetse, "The Family as a System in Conflict", *Journal of Marriage and the Family,* November 1969, pp. 699- 706.

Sprey, Jetse, "On the Management of Conflict in Families", *Journal of Marriage and the Family,* 1971, pp. 722-731.

Szybillc, George J, Sosanie, Arlene K and Tenenbein, Aron, "Should Children Be Seen but Not Heard", *Journal of Advertising Research*, Vol. 17 (December 1977), pp. 7-13.

"The Insider", *The Economic Times: Investor's Guide,* May 15, 2000, p. 8.

Turk, J. L. and W. W. Bell, "Measuring Power in Families", *Journal of Marriage and the Family* (May 1972), pp. 215-222.

Udeshi, Shilpa, "Tracking Competition-No More Picture Perfect Than This", *The Economic Times,* May 17, 2000, p. 8.

"Understanding Consumers", Marketing for Managers, SOM, MS-6, IGNOU.

Vidyarthi, Indrani, "But Seriously, We are the Youth", *The Economic Times: 'Brand Equity'*, April 6, 1999, p.2.

Vijayraghavan, Kala, "White Goods: Cool Fridges are Hottest", *The Economic Times,* June 12, 2000, p.1.

Ward, Scott and Daniel Wackman, "Children Purchase Influence Attempts and Parental Yielding", *Journal of Marketing Research*, Vol. 9 (August 1972), pp. 316-319.

Webster, Cynthia, "Effects of Hispanic Ethnic Identification on Marital Roles in the Purchase Decision Process", *Journal of Consumer Research*, Vol. 21 (September 1994), pp. 319-331.

Wells, William D. and Loscuito, Leonard, "Direct Observation of Purchasing Behaviour", *Journal of Marketing Research*, Vol. 3 (August 1966), pp. 227-233.

Wells, William D. and George Guber, "Life Cycle Concept in Marketing Research", *Journal of Marketing Research*, Vol.3 (November 1966), pp. 355-363.

Wilkie, Robert E., "Husband-Wife Influence in Purchase Decisions - A Confirmation and Extension", *Journal of Marketing Research*, Vol. 12 (May 1975), pp. 224-227.

Wolgast, Elizabeth M., "Do Husbands or Wives Make the Purchasing Decisions", *Journal of Marketing*, Vol. 23 (October 1958), pp. 152-158.